England's Work in India

England's Work in India

BY W. W. HUNTER, C.I.E. LL.D.

GYAN

Published by

Gyan Publishing House
5, Ansari Road
Daryaganj, New Delhi-110002
Phone: 011-47034999, 9811692060
E-mail: books@gyanbooks.com

Distribution Network
gyanbooks.com
India, USA, Canada, UK, Australia

ISBN: 978-93-6208-497-2 (PB)
First Published, 1881

2nd Impression 2024

Printed at: Gyan Press, Delhi.

ENGLAND'S WORK IN INDIA
Author: W. W. HUNTER

England's Work in India.

BY W. W. HUNTER, C.I.E. LL.D.

SMITH, ELDER, & CO. 1881.

PREFACE.

In this little book I try to show what British rule has done for India, and the work which now awaits it. The first two chapters deal with the primary duties of every Government—namely, the protection of its subjects, and the development of the country. The last two chapters treat of what may be called the secondary, but not less important, functions of an Asiatic administration, connected with the food-supply and self-government of the people. The former, when delivered separately as lectures, gave rise to a too favourable, the latter to an unduly despondent, view of our position. I hope, when read together, they will leave behind only a calm resolve, that as Englishmen in time past faithfully did the work which fell to them in India, so Englishmen will now with a firm heart enter on the new duties which are there being forced upon us.

W. W. H.

December 1880.

The Work Done.

The Work to be Done.

ENGLAND'S WORK IN INDIA.

THE WORK DONE.

I. PROTECTION OF PERSON AND PROPERTY.

BRITISH rule in India is again upon its trial. On the one hand, the Government finds itself face to face with problems which, on a much smaller scale in Ireland, are the despair of our wisest statesmen. On the other hand, doubters have arisen who dispute whether our supremacy in the East is a gain either to ourselves or to the peoples over whom we rule. The question as to the benefit of our Indian connection to ourselves is a rhetorical rather than a serious one. For with the downfall of British rule in India would disappear that security of person and property which forms the first essential for our commerce with the East. I, for one, am not afraid of the cry of 'Perish India!' when I remember that that cry means, Perish the greatest customer of England in all the world; perish its chief market for Manchester goods; perish 50 millions sterling of British trade per annum. What we have reason to fear is not the cry of 'Perish India!' but the murmur against the responsibilities which our rule in India involves.

If, however, as some have recently alleged, that rule has failed to benefit the Indian races, then I can sympathize with those who question whether we should extend the responsibilities which Indian rule entails. For no government has a right to exist which does not exist in the interests of the governed. The test of British rule in India is, not what it has done for ourselves, but what it has done for the Indian people. By this test our work in the East must stand or fall. If our attempt to administer that vast and distant empire has turned out a failure; if its people are not more free, more secure, and more prosperous under British rule than they were under their native dynasties; then the wise course for Great Britain would seem to be to curtail her former responsibilities, to accept no new ones, and to withdraw as far as may be from an undertaking to which she had proved unequal.

If, on the other hand, we find that our countrymen have not failed in their splendid and difficult task; if we find that British rule in India means order in place of anarchy, protection by the law instead of oppression by the sword, and a vast free people dwelling in safety where of old each man was beaten down beneath whosoever was stronger than himself, then I think that Great Britain may with a firm heart continue to accept the great responsibility which has fallen to her, and that she may calmly face each new duty which that responsibility involves.

During the last ten years it has been my business to visit, almost every winter, the twelve provinces of India, and to superintend a survey of their population and resources. The Indian Government has, so to speak, ordered me to conduct for it a great stock-taking after a century of British rule. I have often amused myself, during my solitary peregrinations, by imagining what a Hindu of the last century would think of the present state of his country if he could revisit the earth. I have supposed that his first surprise at the outward physical changes had subsided; that he had got accustomed to the fact that thousands of square miles of jungle, which in his time were inhabited only by wild beasts, have been turned into fertile crop-lands; that fever-smitten swamps have been covered with healthy, well-drained cities; that the mountain walls which shut off the interior of India from the seaports have been pierced by roads and scaled by railways; that the great rivers which formed the barriers between provinces, and desolated the country with their floods, have now been controlled to the uses of man, spanned by bridges, and tapped by canals. But what would strike him as more surprising than these outward changes is the security of the people. In provinces where every man, from the prince to the peasant, a hundred years ago, went armed, he would look round in vain for a matchlock or a sword. He would find the multitudinous native states of India, which he remembered in jealous isolation broken only by merciless wars, now trading quietly with each other, bound together by railways and roads, by the post and the telegraph. He would find, moreover, much that was new as well as much that was changed. He would see the country dotted with imposing edifices in a strange foreign architecture, of which he could not guess the uses. He would ask what wealthy prince had reared for himself that spacious palace? He would be answered that the building was no pleasure-house for the rich, but a hospital for the poor. He would inquire, In honour of what new deity is this splendid shrine? He would be told that it was no new temple to the gods, but a school for the people. Instead of bristling fortresses, he would see courts of justice; in place of a Muhammadan general in charge of each district, he would find an English magistrate; instead of a swarming soldiery, he would discover a police.

He would also detect some mournful features in the landscape. In provinces where, a hundred years ago, there was plenty of land for every one who wished to till it, he would see human beings so densely crowded together as to exhaust the soil, and yet fail to wring from it enough to eat. Among a people whose sole means of subsistence was agriculture, he would find a landless proletariate springing up, while millions more were clinging with a despairing grip to their half-acre of earth a-piece, under a burden of rack-rent or usury. On the one hand, he would see great bodies of traders and husbandmen living in a security and comfort unknown in the palmiest days of the Mughals. On the other hand, he would ask himself, as I have often asked myself, whether the prosperity of the prosperous is not highly paid for by the poverty of the poor, and whether this splendid fabric of British rule does not rest deep down on a harder struggle for life.

I shall endeavour to present a few scenes of the panorama which would thus pass before his eyes. There are all the signs at present of a new departure in our dealings with India, and it is of the utmost importance that the English nation should realize the actual facts. My desire is so to state these facts that they may be read and remembered by numbers of my countrymen. It will be in no vainglorious spirit that I contrast what has been with what is. In thinking of her work in India, Great Britain may proudly look back, but she must also look anxiously forward. If, in these preliminary pages, I dwell on what England has accomplished in India, it is only that I may clear the way for stating with the greater emphasis what England has yet to do for the Indian people.

Indian frontier affairs have lately occupied much attention, and I shall commence my sketch by a glance at the frontiers of India in the last century. India is a great three-cornered country, stretching southward from Asia into the sea. Its northern base rests upon the Himalayan ranges; the chief part of its western side is washed by the Indian Ocean, and of its eastern by the Bay of Bengal. But while thus guarded along the whole length of its boundaries by Nature's defences, the mountains and the sea, it has, at its north-eastern and north-western corners, two opposite sets of gateways which connect it with the rest of Asia. Through these gateways, successive hordes of invaders have poured into India, and in the last century the process was still going on. Each set of new-comers plundered and massacred without mercy and without restraint. During 700 years, the warring races of Central Asia and Afghanistan filled up their measure of bloodshed and pillage to the full. Sometimes they returned with their spoil to their mountains, leaving desolation behind; sometimes they killed off or drove out the former inhabitants, and settled down in India as lords of the soil; sometimes they founded imperial dynasties, destined to be crushed, each in its turn, by a new host swarming into India through the Afghan passes. In the middle of the last century, six such inroads on a great scale took place in twenty-three years. The first was led by a soldier of fortune from Persia, who slaughtered Afghan and Indian alike; the last five were regular Afghan invasions.

The precise meaning of the word invasion in India during the last century, may be gathered from the following facts. It signified not merely a host of twenty to a hundred thousand barbarians on the march, paying for nothing, and eating up every town, and cottage, and farmyard; burning and slaughtering on the slightest provocation, and often in mere sport. It usually also meant a grand final sack and massacre at the capital of the invaded country. Here is the account of the fate of Delhi in the first of the six invasions in the middle of the last century—an account drawn up by the least rhetorical and most philosophical of Indian historians, the father of John Stuart Mill. Delhi had peacefully opened its gates to the strangers, but a brawl had afterwards arisen between the troops and the citizens. 'With the first light of the morning,' the invading leader, 'Nadir, issued forth, and, dispersing bands of soldiers in every direction, ordered them to slaughter the inhabitants, without regard to age or sex, in every street or avenue in which the body of a murdered Persian should be found. From sunrise to midday the sabre raged; and by that time not less than 8000 were numbered with the dead. During the massacre and pillage the city was set on fire in several places.' At the end of a fifty-eight days' sack, the plunderers went off with their booty, leaving the capital stripped, burned, and desolate.

On this first of the six invasions, then, 8000 men, women, and children were hacked to pieces in one forenoon in the streets of the capital. But the Persian general knew how to stop the massacre at his pleasure. The Afghan leaders had less authority, and their five great invasions during the thirteen middle years of the last century form one of the most appalling tales of bloodshed and wanton cruelty ever inflicted on the human race. In one of these invasions, the miserable capital, Delhi, again opened her gates and received the Afghans as guests. Yet for several weeks, not merely for six hours on this occasion, the citizens were exposed to every foul enormity which a barbarian army could practise on a prostrate foe. Meanwhile the Afghan cavalry were scouring the country, slaying, burning, and mutilating in the meanest hamlet as in the greatest town. They took especial delight in sacking the holy places of the Hindus, and murdering the defenceless votaries at the shrines. For example, one gang of 25,000 Afghan horsemen swooped down upon the sacred city of Muttra during a festival, while it was thronged with peaceful Hindu pilgrims engaged in their devotions. 'They burned the houses,' says the Tyrolese Jesuit Tieffenthaler, who was in India at that time, 'together with their inmates, slaughtering others with the sword and the lance; hauling off into captivity maidens and youths, men and women. In the temples they slaughtered cows,' the sacred animal of the Hindus, 'and smeared the images and pavement with the blood.'

It is needless to quote further from the tale of Afghan atrocities in the last century. They went on year after year, the Afghans being too loosely organized to serve as a barrier against the hosts from Central Asia, and always ready for an Indian invasion on their own account. The border-land between Afghanistan and India lay silent and waste; indeed, districts far within the frontier, which had once been densely inhabited, and which are now again thickly peopled, were swept bare of inhabitants. Thus Gujránwála, the seat of the ancient capital of the Punjab in Buddhist times, was utterly depopulated. Its present inhabitants are immigrants of comparatively recent date. The district, which was thus stripped of its inhabitants in the last century, has now a new population of over half a million souls. The Afghan question survives to this day, but its present form, although by no means easy of solution, is preferable to the shape in which it presented itself in the last century.

In the last century, however, invasions and inroads were yearly events along the whole frontier of India. The Himalayan mountains, instead of serving as a northern wall to shut out aggressors, formed a line of fastnesses from which the hill races poured down upon the plains. For fifteen hundred miles along their base stretched a thick belt of territory which no one dared to cultivate. This silent border-land varied from twenty to fifty miles in breadth, and embraced a total area of 30,000 square miles, that yielded no food for man, but teemed with wild beasts, which nightly sallied forth to ravage the herds and hamlets in the open country beyond. Such a border-land seemed to the miserable villagers on the plains to be the best possible frontier; for its dense jungles served as some sort of barrier against the invasions of the wild Himalayan races, and it bred deadly fevers which made havoc of armies that attempted a passage through it. Indeed, the ancient Hindu laws of Manu, written more than 2000 years ago, ordained, as a protection to a royal city or kingdom, a belt of wilderness twenty miles around it in place of fortifications; and the peasantry of Northern India were thankful in the last century for the tract of disease-laden jungle which, to a certain extent, defended them from the savage hillmen beyond.

Such was the state of the north-western and the long northern boundary of India before the establishment of British rule. A glance at the north-eastern border discloses a still more painful picture. The history of the fertile valley of Assam, in the north-eastern corner of India, is one long narrative of invasion and extermination. Anciently the seat of a powerful Hindu kingdom, whose ruined forts of massive hewn stone we find buried in the jungle, Assam was devastated, like the rest of Eastern Bengal, by the fanatical Muhammadan invaders in the fifteenth century from the west. A fierce aboriginal race (the Koch) next swooped down on it from the north. They in turn were crushed by another aboriginal race (the Ahams) from the east; and these again were being exterminated by the Burmese from the south, when they implored the English to interfere. During the last century, large tracts of Assam were depopulated, and throughout that province and Eastern Bengal 30,000 square miles of fertile frontier districts lay waste. In addition to these systematic invasions, the smaller hill tribes every autumn rushed down upon the miserable hamlets which were left, and drove away the women and the cattle.

The great mountain wall round Northern India failed therefore, till the British came upon the scene, to afford any security to the Indian races. The sea, which forms the natural defence of the rest of the country, was in like manner only a source of new dangers. On the Bay of Bengal, the pirates from the Burmese coast sailed up the great rivers, burning the villages, massacring or carrying off into slavery the inhabitants. The first English surveyor, in the second half of the last century, entered on his maps a fertile and now populous tract of a thousand square miles on the sea-board, as bare of villages, with the significant words written across it, 'Depopulated by the Maghs,' or sea-robbers. A fleet was ineffectually maintained by the Muhammadan Government to keep open the river channels, and a heavy impost, whose name survives to the present day, although the tax itself has long been abolished, was in vain levied for this service. On the other side of the peninsula in the Indian Ocean, piracy was conducted on a grander scale. Wealthy rájás kept up luxurious courts upon the extortions which their pirate fleets levied from trading vessels, and from the villages along the coast. The truth is, that the natural defences of India, the mountains and the sea, were in the last century equally powerless to protect the Indian races.

This state of things could not be permitted under British rule, and the first business of the English was to secure India from foreign invasions. The sea-robbers were effectively dealt with. One of Clive's achievements was rooting out the pirate nests of the south-western coast; and the Indian navy, after sweeping the robber hordes from the sea, and rendering Indian waters as safe as the English Channel, finished its work nineteen years ago, and was abolished in 1861. The unruly tribes of the Himalayan frontiers had always their hill fastnesses to retreat to. Their subjugation took a longer time, and is less complete, as our troubles with

Afghanistan still attest. But by persuasion, and, when necessary, by chastisement, we have taught the wild races along the whole northern and north-eastern frontier, for a distance of 1500 miles, the lesson that they must please keep quiet, and betake themselves to some other livelihood than the pillage of the husbandmen on the plains. Most of them have proved apt scholars. The great kingdom of Nepal on the north, which forced us to correct its inveterate practice of raiding by two campaigns, followed by partial annexation, has, for the last sixty years, been our firm ally, and hurried out its armies to our help in the Mutiny of 1857. At one time during this long interval, the dynastic intrigues, always fermenting in a native court, threatened to bring the Nepalese into conflict with the British; and on that occasion the whole kingdom of Nepal was kept loyal to its treaties, through a prolonged crisis, by the firmness and skill of a single Englishman, Brian Hodgson. Other native states, like the principality of Kuch Behar, at once settled down into peaceful industry. Its first and only treaty with us, dated 1773, remains unbroken by either party to this day, a monument of mutual good faith.

A firm frontier being established in Northern India, the peasantry spread themselves out upon the unoccupied border lands. The task of reclaiming these tracts has been a heavy one. In some parts, as in the now prosperous district of Goalpara with its half-million of inhabitants, more money was spent, until twenty-five years ago, by Government in rewards for killing the wild animals than the whole sum realized from the land revenue. This broad belt of waste land along the frontier was almost the only unoccupied territory which the British Government could grant to European settlers. The first British capitalists had to do battle alike with the banditti and the wild beasts. We read in the manuscript records of 1788 of a Mr. Raush, one of the earliest English merchants in Assam, who made an alliance on his own account with the local rájá, and sent a private regiment of 700 men to the aid of that prince. While the natives of India have pushed their rice cultivation towards the foot of the mountains, English capitalists have dotted their slopes with tea-plantations. Not less than 13,000 square miles of border-districts have been reclaimed, and yield each year at the lowest estimate eighteen millions sterling worth of produce. The tea-gardens alone exported last year three millions sterling worth of tea, chiefly to England.

The unsettled frontier of the last century, meant that sixty thousand square miles of border-land (double the whole area of Scotland), were abandoned to jungle and the wild beasts, not because there were no people to cultivate the soil, but because they did not dare to do so. It signified that tracts which might have yielded, and which will yet yield, thirty millions sterling worth of food each year, lay untilled through terror of the turbulent hill races. The security given by a century of British rule in these frontier districts means 13,000 square miles already brought under the plough, growing each year eighteen millions sterling worth of produce, or more than the average normal cost of the Indian army and the whole defence of the Indian Empire.

The task of freeing India from foreign invasion was, however, only the first of many heavy responsibilities which our acquisition of the country entailed. The dying throes of the Mughal Empire had let loose its disbanded or revolted armies upon the people. The troops, finding that their pay was no longer forthcoming from the Muhammadan treasury, lived by open pillage. In what are now the most peaceful and most populous districts of Bengal, there were, in the last century, standing camps of banditti. Many of the principal native families, being ruined by the exactions of the Musalmán tax-gatherers, betook themselves to plunder. They sheltered the banditti on their estates, levied black-mail from the surrounding villages as the price of immunity from depredation, and shared in the pillage of such as would not come to terms. Their country-houses were robber-strongholds, and the English judges of the last century have left it on record that a gang-robbery never occurred without a landed proprietor being at the bottom of it.

Lawlessness breeds lawlessness, and the miserable peasants, stripped of their little hoards, were forced to become plunderers in their turn. Many 'husbandmen,' says an official report of 1771, 'who have hitherto borne the first of characters among their neighbours, pursue this last resource to procure themselves a subsistence.' The Council at Calcutta reported in 1772 that organized gangs of robbers were burning, plundering, and ravaging the interior districts of Bengal in bodies of 50,000 men. The English found no police in India to cope with this great evil. Each village had its watchman, but the village watchman would have been powerless against the robber-gangs, and so he entered into league with them. For a time the East India Company's troops were constantly engaged against the banditti. In 1773 we hear of our Sepoys 'being totally defeated' by a robber horde, and 'their English leader with the whole party cut off.' But by degrees these vast armies of banditti were broken up, and scattered themselves over the country in smaller gangs.

Such lawlessness was the normal condition of all India for a full half-century, and in some provinces for many centuries, before the advent of British rule. A long succession of invaders during 700 years had crushed beneath them the preceding races. In many instances, the previous inhabitants were driven from their fields altogether and forced to take refuge in the mountains or jungles. They then became what is called in India a 'depressed race,' or a 'predatory caste.' In every province we find one or more of these depressed or vanquished races, such as the Bhars of Oudh, the Bhíls of Jalaun, the Gaulis of the Central Provinces, the Chandels and Bundelas of Bundelkhand, the Ahams of Assam, besides the numerous hill tribes scattered over the country. In the last century, there were over a hundred hereditary 'predatory castes' or marauding hill and forest tribes in India, and many of their names survive to our days in the census of 1871; that is to say, there were more than one hundred resolute communities openly living from generation to generation by plunder.

Here, then, was a great organization of the criminal classes, which had long existed, and which the English had to put down without the aid of any regular police. At first the Company's servants attempted to extirpate crime by copying the cruel criminal code of the Musalmans. Warren Hastings, for example, made a law that every convicted gang-robber should be executed; that he should be executed in all the forms and terrors of the native law in his own village; that his whole family should be made slaves, and that every inhabitant of the village should be fined. The gang-robbers retaliated by incendiarism on a great scale throughout the country. In 1780 they were believed to have caused the conflagration of Calcutta which burned down 15,000 houses. Nearly 200 people perished in the flames. 'Deduct,' saith the deed for the Benares District for the year 1782, 'deduct the devastations, etc., of two months' disturbances, *sicca* rupees 666,666,' or over £70,000. 'A few nights ago,' says a Calcutta newspaper of 1780, 'four armed men entered the house of a Moorman, near Chowringhi,' the principal street, 'and carried off his daughter.' No native ever ventured out after dusk with a good shawl on; and it was the invariable practice, even in English mansions in Calcutta, for the porter to lock the outer door at the commencement of each meal, and not to open it again till the butler brought him word that the plate was safely shut up in its strong box.

Clear cases of fire-raising are constantly recorded, and at length it was gravely recommended 'that all those owning straw houses should have a long bamboo with three hooks at the end to catch the villains.'

All this has changed. Strange as it may sound, there is now less crime in India than in England. For each million persons in England and Wales there are about 870 criminals always in gaol. In India, where the police is very completely organized, there are only 614 prisoners in gaol for each million of the people. Moreover, in England and Wales there are 340 women in gaol for each million of the female population, while in India they have only twenty-eight women in gaol for each million of the female population. The petty offences, punished by a fine, are also less numerous in Bengal than in England, compared with the total number of inhabitants. These gaol returns are sometimes misleading, owing to differences in the class of punishment inflicted, but I have satisfied myself that the above figures substantially represent the facts. The use of troops against banditti is now a thing of the past. The existence of an army is less realised in a rural district of Bengal than in an English shire. Of the sixty-three millions of people in that province, probably forty millions go through life without ever seeing the face of a soldier.

A century of British rule has, therefore, not only secured the Indian frontier from invaders, but it has freed the interior of India from banditti. How has this result been achieved? Partly by legislation and partly by police. The English in India recognised the fact that they had a special class of crimes to deal with, and they framed a special department of criminal law to put those crimes down. 'The *dakaits* or gang-robbers of Bengal,' so runs a State paper written in 1772, 'are not, like the robbers of England, individuals driven to such desperate courses by sudden want. They are robbers by profession and even by birth. They are formed into regular communities, and their families subsist by the spoils which they bring home to them.' These spoils were frequently brought from great distances; and peaceful villages 300 miles up the Ganges lived by housebreaking in Calcutta. A special law was therefore framed against the crime of *dakaiti*, or gang-robbery, that is to say, robbery committed by five or more persons. Another special crime was *thagi*, or strangling dexterously performed by bands of professional murderers disguised as travelling merchants or pilgrims. The *thags* and *dakaits*, or hereditary stranglers and gang-robbers, thought none the worse of themselves for their profession, and were regarded by their countrymen with an awe which in the last century could hardly be distinguished from respect. 'I am a *thag* or strangler of the Royal Records,' one of these gentlemen was good enough to explain to an English officer: 'I and my fathers have been professional stranglers for twenty generations.' Accordingly special laws were framed to deal with the crime of 'being a *thag*' or professional strangler.

Special laws, however, would have done very little

without special police. A separate department of the criminal administration was therefore created to deal with these widespread special crimes of India. It has effectively done its work. Some time ago, I was taken to visit the principal gaol of one of the Indian provinces. At parting, when I was thanking the governor of the prison for all he had shown me, he exclaimed: 'Ah! there is one thing more we must not forget to see.' He took me to a well-ventilated, comfortable room in the gaol hospital, where, lolling upon pillows, reclined a reverend, white-bearded man. 'This,' he said, 'is the last of our *thags*. He alone survives of the batch which we received twenty-five years ago.' I found that the venerable strangler had been for fifteen years enjoying himself in the hospital, the object of much solicitude to the doctors, and his life carefully prolonged by medical comforts, as an interesting relic of the past.

Nevertheless, this problem also presents itself from time to time, although in a mitigated form. The old predatory castes, the survivals of down-trodden, half-exterminated races under the native dynasties, still cling to their wandering life. But most of them, like the Bediyas, are now merely gipsy families, who roam from village to village, earning a little rice by their singing and juggling, or by their dexterity as bird-catchers, basket-weavers, and fortune-tellers. Their boldest flight in robbery is the pilfering of a stray chicken or kid. In recently annexed parts of India, however, as in the province of Oudh, the old predatory clans still give trouble. A special law, entitled the

Criminal Tribes Act, has accordingly been levelled against them, and is occasionally enforced. For example, in the Gonda district of Oudh, which passed under British rule only in 1855, there is a caste of professional thieves called Barwárs. They spread over the country in communities of forty or fifty, and have no objection to rob temples, but will not steal cattle. They go on more distant expeditions in parties of two or three. Their plunder is fairly divided, a portion being set apart to buy offerings of goats and ardent spirits to their patron goddess, and a fixed percentage being paid to the landholder of the village. They carry on their trade with hereditary skill; but the rules of their religion sternly restrict their operations to the daytime, between sunrise and sunset. Any Barwár stealing by night is ignominiously turned out of the caste. In 1869, these scrupulous gentlemen numbered 2500 in a single *pargana* or parish. But they have, under British rule, sunk from their ancient dignity as a hereditary robber-community, and, like my old friend the professional strangler in the gaol hospital, they are regarded with much interest by the local authorities as a relic of the past. They have been placed under the operation of the Criminal Tribes Act, and are now betaking themselves to the more commonplace callings of small husbandmen and petty pilferers. Throughout almost the whole of British India the ancient special crimes have been extirpated. The old criminal tribes find it more profitable to be on the side of the law than against it, and now seek employment as detectives or house-watchmen. We have seen how the Indian navy, after having swept the sea of piracy and cleared out the robber-nests at the river mouths, finished its work, and was abolished nineteen years ago. In like manner, the old lawlessness in the interior has now disappeared, and the special branch of the criminal administration known as the *Thagi* and *Dakaiti* or Stranglers' and Gang-robbers' Department, has practically ceased from its operations in British India.

We have of late years heard a great deal about Indian famines. The heart of England has been touched by tales of suffering and privation on a vast scale, and the charity of England has flowed forth on a scale equally munificent. Famine is now recognised as one of the most difficult problems with which the Indian Administration has to deal. A hundred years ago it was regarded not as a problem of administration, but as a visitation of God utterly beyond the control of man. When the rains, on which the crops depended, fell short, no crops were reared, and the people perished. Sometimes their failure was confined to a single district, and only a few thousand families starved to death. Sometimes their failure extended to a province, and the victims were counted by hundreds of thousands. More rarely the rains failed over a still greater area, and, as in 1770, a third of the whole population perished. The loss of life was accepted in each case as a natural and an inevitable consequence of the loss of the crop. The earth had yielded no food, and so the people, in the ordinary and legitimate course of things, died. The famine of 1837 left behind so terrible a memory, that to this day the peasants of Hamirpur employ it as an era by which to calculate their ages. Such calamities are accepted as the ordinary and inevitable visitations of Providence in Asia. It is said that the recent famine in Northern China stripped large tracts of one-half their inhabitants.

Here is a bird's-eye view of a single famine in the last century, taken almost word for word from the official records. 'The fields of rice,' one of the native superintendents of Bengal reported in the autumn of 1769, 'are become like fields of dried straw.' 'The mortality,' wrote the President of the Bengal Council in the following spring—'the mortality, the beggary exceed all description. Above one-third of the inhabitants have perished in the once plentiful province of Purniah, and in other parts the misery is equal.' All through the stifling summer of 1770 the people went on dying. The husbandmen sold their cattle; they sold their implements of agriculture; they devoured their seed-grain; they sold their sons and daughters, till at length no buyer of children could be found; they ate the leaves of trees and the grass of the field; and in June 1770, the Resident at the Darbar affirmed that the living were feeding on the dead. Day and night a torrent of famished and disease-stricken wretches poured into the great cities. At an early period of the year, pestilence had broken out. In March we find small-pox at Murshidábád, where it glided through the viceregal guards, and cut off the Prince Saífat in his palace. The streets were blocked up with promiscuous heaps of the dying and dead. Interment could not do its work quick enough; even the dogs and jackals, the public scavengers of the East, became unable to accomplish their revolting work, and the multitude of mangled and festering corpses at length threatened the existence of the citizens.

Two years after the dearth, Warren Hastings made a progress through Bengal, and he deliberately states the loss to have been 'at least one-third of the inhabitants,' or probably about ten millions of people. Nineteen years later, the next Governor-General, Lord Cornwallis, had still to report to the Court of Directors that one-third of the Company's territory in Bengal was 'a jungle inhabited only by wild beasts.'

In that terrible summer of 1770, in which ten millions of peasants perished, only £9000 were distributed to aid the starving population of Bengal. A century later, in the much milder Bengal scarcity of 1874, the British Government spent close on four millions sterling, and during the five years ending 1878, it devoted over fourteen millions sterling in feeding its people during famine. Here is one great difference between the last century and the present one. But it is by no means the most important difference. In the last century, neither the Government nor the people thought that it was possible to deal with a great Indian famine. Any such efforts were, in the words of the Bengali proverb, merely *watering the top of a tree whose roots are cut*. In the present century, earnest efforts have been made to bring famine within administrative control. A vast organization of preventive and remedial agencies is constantly kept in readiness to deal with the periodically recurring dearths.

Canals, irrigation works of many kinds, railways, roads, steamboats, and every improved form of modern communication, together with State charity in India and the munificent benevolence of the British nation at home,—these are the weapons with which the Indian Government now does battle against famine.

That battle is not yet won. Many Indian administrators of great experience, both English and native, still believe that, when a real famine has once developed itself, it is impossible to prevent a terrible loss of life. This is a subject which will require very faithful dealing. The temptation in modern times is not to grudge State aid during famine, but to lavish the public funds with an open hand, so that each official may be able to say that nothing which money could accomplish for the starving population was left undone. The problem of Indian famine is still unsolved; but it has been accepted by all earnest administrators as one for which we must find a solution. The famine of 1877 and 1878 is supposed to have raised the mortality from 35 to 63 per thousand, causing from disease and starvation throughout all India an excess of 5¼ million deaths. But the cultivated area in the stricken tracts was greater, by 120,000 acres, after the famine than before it. Heartrending as was the calamity, it produced no results analogous to those of famines in the last century and early years of the present one, when 'half the *ryots* were credibly reported to have perished,' when the landed classes were completely disorganized, and a third of the land relapsed into jungle.

The effect of famine in modern times upon the growth

of the population is almost imperceptible. Taking the whole scarcities of the past thirty years, the Commissioners estimate the annual deaths from the diseases and all other causes connected with famine at 'less than 2 per 1000' of the inhabitants. Permanent depopulation from any cause is now unknown. No frontier belt is left waste through fear of invasions from the north, no provinces are swept clean by Marhatta cavalry from the south, no villages are laid waste by internal banditti, and no districts are now stripped of inhabitants by famine. In the last century all these causes of depopulation were at work. The quick-growing jungle spread over the deserted land, and the fierce beasts of the tropics were the undisputed lords of fertile tracts. In the old revenue accounts of the native Government during the last century, there was a column in each district for *paldtika* or deserted lands, literally 'the lands from which the people had fled.' Even ten years after the famine of 1770, a once populous district was a silent jungle; and in 1780 a small body of Sepoys could with difficulty force its way through its forests. 'For 120 miles,' says an eye-witness, 'they marched through but an extensive wood, all the way a perfect wilderness; sometimes a small village presented itself in the midst of these jungles, with a little cultivated ground around it, hardly sufficient to encamp the two battalions. These woods abound with tigers and bears, which infested the camp every night, but did no other damage than carrying off a child and killing some of the gentlemen's baggage-bullocks.'

As the rural communities relinquished their hamlets

and drew closer together towards the centre of a district, the wild beasts pressed hungrily on their rear. In vain the East India Company offered a reward for each tiger's head sufficient to maintain a peasant's family in comfort for three months—an item of outlay which our officers deemed so important, that when, in the financial crisis of 1790–91, the Treasury had to suspend all payments, it made the tiger-money and diet allowance for prisoners the sole exceptions to the rule. In vain it spent the whole land-revenue of a frontier district in rewards for killing wild beasts. A belt of jungle filled with ferocious animals lay for years around the cultivated land. The official records frequently speak of the mail-bag being carried off by tigers, and the custom of the mail-runners carrying a bell to scare away the wild beasts survived to our own day. Lord Cornwallis, in 1789, had to sanction a grant of public money to free the military road through Bengal from the depredations of these animals.

The ravages of the wild elephants were on a larger scale, and their extermination formed one of the most important duties of the British officers after the country passed under our rule. Tigers, leopards, and wolves slew their thousands of men and their hundreds of thousands of cattle. But the herd of wild elephants was absolutely resistless, lifting off roofs, pushing down walls, trampling a village under foot as if it were a city of sand which a child had built upon the shore. In two parishes alone, during the last few years of the native administration, fifty-six hamlets with their surrounding lands 'had all been destroyed and gone to jungle, caused by the depredations of wild elephants.' Another official return states that forty market villages throughout Bírbhúm district had been deserted from the same cause. Large reductions had to be made in the land-tax, and the East India Company borrowed tame elephants from the native Viceroy's stud in order to catch the wild ones. 'I had ocular proof on my journey,' writes an English officer in 1791, 'of their ravages. The poor timid native ties his cot in a tree, to which he retires when the elephants approach, and silently views the destruction of his cottage and the whole profits of his labour.' 'One night,' writes an English surveyor in 1810, 'although I had a guard, the men of the village close to my tent retired to the trees, and the women hid themselves among the cattle, leaving their huts a prey to the elephants, who know very well where to look for grain. Two nights before, some of them had unroofed a hut in the village, and had eaten up all the grain which a poor family possessed.' 'Most fortunately for the population of the country,' wrote the greatest elephant-hunter of the last century, 'they delight in the sequestered range of the mountains; if they preferred the plains, whole kingdoms would be laid waste.'

All this is now changed. One of the complaints of the modern Englishman in India is that he can so seldom get a shot at a tiger. Wolves are dying out in many provinces; the ancient Indian lion has disappeared. The wild elephant is so rare that he is specially protected by the Government, and in most parts of India he can only be caught by official licence and under official supervision. Many districts have petitioned for a close season, so as to preserve the edible game still remaining. The only animal that has defied the energy of the British official is the snake. One may, however, judge of the loss of life by wild beasts in the last century from the deaths caused by this, their chief survivor at the present day. The ascertained number of persons who died from snake-bite in 1875 was 17,000, out of a total of 21,391 killed by snakes and all other wild animals. The deaths from wild beasts in the last century were probably not under 150,000 a year.

I shall now briefly summarize some of the outward and obvious results of a century of British rule. As regards the northern or Himalayan frontier of India, the wild hill tribes are no longer invaders, but are employed as loyal soldiers or border police. As regards the southern frontier of India, the sea, the pirate races have been converted into cheap and excellent seamen. Indian waters are now as safe as the English Channel, and the Indian navy, having finished its work, is disbanded. As regards internal disturbances, banditti are unknown, breaches of the law are rarer in India than in England, and the special department which was created to deal with the old special crimes of India now finds no more work to do within the British provinces. Famine, which in the last century was considered as the act of God, beyond any help of man, has been accepted as the great administrative problem of our day; and a vast organization of public works, State relief, and private charity, is interposed between the Indian races and the merciless calamities of nature. As regards the reclamation of waste land, formerly the local hero was the man who cut down the jungle; now a special branch of legislation is required to enable the Government to conserve what jungle remains, and to plant fresh forests. These are a few of the outward and visible results of a century of British rule in India.

II. DEVELOPMENT OF THE COUNTRY AND ITS PEOPLE.

THERE are other and less obvious results of British rule; and perhaps foremost among them is the development of new industries and the growth of great centres of trade. Commercial cities, in our sense of the word, did not exist in ancient India. The capital was the standing camp of the monarch; its trade depended upon the presence of the court. Magnificent emperors required magnificent cities around them, and an inconsiderate or a tyrannical prince ordered the movements of the citizens as he ordered the movements of his troops. One cruel emperor of the house of Tughlak forced the whole inhabitants of Delhi, in the north of India, to migrate to his new capital, Daulatábád, 700 miles away in the distant south. Thousands perished on the road. The king twice changed his mind. Twice he allowed the miserable people to return to Delhi; twice he compelled them on pain of death to leave it. One of these forced migrations took place during a famine; a great part of the citizens died of hunger; the rest were utterly ruined. But, says the historian, 'the emperor's orders were strictly complied with, and the ancient capital was left desolate.'

A large external trade was indeed an impossibility at

the native metropolis, Delhi, which lay more than a thousand miles from the river's mouth. But even the capitals of the sea-board provinces were chosen for military purposes, and with small regard to the commercial capabilities of their situation. Thus, in Lower Bengal, the Muhammadans under different dynasties fixed in succession on six towns as their capital. Each of these successive capitals was on a river bank; but not one of them possessed any foreign trade, nor indeed could have been approached by an old East Indiaman. They were simply the court and camp of the king or the viceroy for the time being. Colonies of skilful artisans settled round the palaces of the nobles to supply the luxurious fabrics of oriental life. After the prince and court had in some new caprice abandoned the city, the artisans remained, and a little settlement of weavers was often the sole surviving proof that the decaying town had once been a capital city. Thus the exquisite muslins of Dacca and the soft silks of Murshidábád still bear witness to the days when these two places were successively the capital of Bengal. The artisans worked in their own houses. The manufactures of India were essentially domestic industries, conducted by special castes, each member of which wove at his own hereditary loom, and in his own village or homestead.

One of the earliest results of British rule in India was the growth of great mercantile towns. Our rule derived its origin from our commerce, and from the first the East India Company's efforts were directed to creating centres for maritime trade. Other European nations, the Portuguese, the Dutch, the Danes, and the French, have rivalled us as merchants and conquerors in India, and each of them in turn attempted to found great seaports. The long Indian coast, both on the east and the west, is dotted with decaying villages which were once the busy scenes of those nations' early European trade. Of all their famous capitals in India, not one has now the commercial importance of Cardiff or Greenock, and not one of them has a harbour which would admit at low tide a ship drawing 20 feet.

The truth is that it is far easier to pitch a camp and erect a palace, which, under the native dynasties, was synonymous with founding a capital, than it is to create a centre of trade. Such centres must grow of themselves, and cannot be called suddenly into existence by the fiat of the wisest autocrat. It is in this difficult enterprise, in which the Portuguese, the Dutch, the Danes, and the French had successively failed, that the British in India have succeeded. We make our appearance in the long list of races who have ruled that splendid empire, not as temple-builders like the Hindus, nor as palace and tomb-builders like the Musalmáns, nor as fort-builders like the Marhattas, nor as church-builders like the Portuguese, but in the more commonplace capacity of town-builders, as a nation that had the talent for selecting sites on which great commercial cities would grow up, and who have in this way created a new industrial life for the Indian people.

Calcutta and Bombay, the two commercial capitals of India, are essentially the creations of British rule.

Shortly after Bombay was ceded by the Portuguese to the British Crown in 1661, as part of the dower of the wife of Charles II., the king was glad to hand over his unprofitable acquisition, which was then considered the grave of Europeans, to a company of London merchants for an annual payment of £10 in gold. Bombay city has now close on three-quarters of a million of inhabitants, living entirely by commerce. It ranks next to London (if we except Calcutta and its municipal suburbs) in the cities of the British Empire. Its population is nearly one and a half times that of Glasgow or Liverpool, and nearly double that of Manchester or Birmingham.

The history of Calcutta, the metropolis of India, is still more striking. Together with its municipal suburbs, it has a population exceeding three-quarters of a million, or nearly double that of any city in Great Britain except London. Less than two centuries ago, when our countrymen first settled at Calcutta, they were a poor band of fugitive merchants seeking shelter from the extortions of the native ruler of Bengal; and the future City of Palaces consisted of three clusters of mud huts on the river bank. It was not their first attempt to found a city where they could trade in peace. The sea-board of Bengal was the scene of many an earlier and unsuccessful effort. Sometimes the English were driven away by the exactions of the native general in charge of the surrounding district; sometimes the river on which their little town was rising shifted its course, and left their wharves high and dry; sometimes the estuary which they had fixed upon as a harbour silted up, and long banks of sand rose between their port and the sea. Calcutta on the eastern coast of India, and Bombay on the west, are the results of a long and patient series of unsuccessful efforts—they represent the survival of the fittest; and many an English heart was broken, and many a hard-earned fortune lost, in attempting to found ports at the mouths of silting rivers, and amid the dismal Bengal swamps, before Calcutta rose to its proud position, next to London, as the metropolis of India and the second city of the British Empire.

In one of these deserted seats of the early British trade, I have seen the husbandman driving his plough over what were once the wet docks, and turning up spars and rotten fragments of sloops from the furrows. Others of them have entirely disappeared from the map. For example, the harbour on the Orissa sea-board, which was officially reported, as late as 1809, to be the safest and most frequented port on that coast, has now ceased to exist. The mouth of the river has so completely silted up, and is so perfectly concealed by a dense fringe of jungle, that it is almost impossible for a strange vessel to discover it. A similar ruin has, in a milder degree, fallen on every ancient seaport of India. All round the Indian coast, from the Gulf of Cambay to the mouths of the Irawadi, the silt-bearing rivers and the sand-charged tides have built up barriers of mud between the old historic harbours and modern commerce.

This fate would long ago have overtaken Calcutta but for the strenuous efforts of our countrymen. The Húglí river, upon which Calcutta lies, forms one of the chief mouths of the Ganges. Six great historical ports have been built upon its banks. The oldest of them, Sátgáon, the ancient royal port of Bengal under the native dynasties, has been completely deserted by the navigable channel, and is now a thatched village crumbling upon the banks of a muddy ditch. The Dutch, the French, and the Danes each set up capitals and ports of their own on the Húglí river, off which vessels of the largest tonnage in the last century used to lie. Every one of these once famous emporiums is now blocked up by banks of sand and silt, and is unapproachable by sea-going ships at the present day.

Calcutta has been saved from the same isolation by a system of river-engineering which forms one of the memorable triumphs in the contest of man with nature. The river Húglí has ceased to be the direct channel of the Ganges; but Calcutta alone, of all the successive river capitals of Bengal, has overcome the difficulties incident to its position as a deltaic centre of commerce. Strenuous efforts of engineering are required to keep open the three offshoots of the Ganges above Calcutta which combine to form the Húglí. Still greater watchfulness and more extensive operations are demanded by the eighty miles of the Húglí itself below Calcutta, to save it from the fate of other deltaic streams, and to prevent it from silting up. In 1853, the deterioration of the Húglí channel led to a proposal to found an auxiliary port to Calcutta on the Matlá, another mouth of the Ganges farther east. A committee then appointed to inquire into the subject reported that 'the river Húglí was deteriorating gradually and progressively.' At that time 'science had done nothing to aid in facilities for navigation;' but since then, everything has been effected which the foresight of modern engineering could suggest or the power of modern capital could achieve. Observations on the condition of the Húglí channels are taken hourly, gigantic steam-dredgers are continually at work, and the shifting of the shoals is carefully recorded. By these means the port of Calcutta has been kept open for ships of the largest tonnage, drawing 26 feet, and almost seems to have outlived the danger which threatened its existence.

I have dwelt on the rise of our commercial capitals in India, because the development of city life in India means the growth of a new industrial career for the people. Formerly, as we have seen, the industries of India were essentially domestic manufactures, each man working at his hereditary occupation, at his own loom or at his own forge. Under British rule a new era of production has arisen in India—an era of production on a great scale based upon the co-operation of capital and labour, in place of the small household manufactures of ancient times. To us, who have from our youth grown up in the midst of a keen commercial civilisation, it is not easy to realize the change thus implied. I shall briefly indicate some of the most salient features of the revolution which it has wrought in the industrial life of the Indian people.

The great industrial cities of British India are the

type of the new state of things implied by this change. Under native rule, the country had reached what political economists of Mill's school called 'the stationary stage' of civilisation. The husbandmen simply raised the food-grains necessary to feed them from one harvest to another. If the food crops failed in any district, the local population had no capital and no other crops wherewith to buy food from other districts; so, in the natural and inevitable course of things, they perished. Now the peasants of India raise other and far more profitable crops than the mere food-stuffs on which they live. They also raise an annual surplus of grain for exportation, which is available for India's own wants in time of need; and there is a much larger aggregate of capital in the country, that is to say, a much greater national reserve or staying power. The so-called 'stationary stage' in India has disappeared, and the Indian peasant is keenly alive to each new demand which the market of the world may make upon the industrial capabilities of his country.

Thus, up to 1850, cotton was produced on a small scale in India, and the total value exported averaged during the previous five years only $1\frac{3}{4}$ millions sterling. Ten years later, the American war gave rise to a sudden demand; and the Indian cotton exports rushed up, till, in 1865, they exceeded the enormous value of $37\frac{3}{4}$ millions sterling. This vast amount of money went into the pockets of the cultivators, who, the moment that they had found a more profitable crop than their old food-stuffs, quickly began to cultivate it on a large scale. What the American war was to the Bombay peasant, the Russian war had been to the Bengal husbandman. The blockade of the Baltic ports put an end to Great Britain's supply of fibres from Russia during the Crimean campaign. Forthwith the Bengal peasant enormously increased his production of jute. In 1852–53, before the Crimean war, the whole export of jute from Bengal was about £100,000. In 1872–73, it exceeded 4¼ millions sterling, an increase of fortyfold.

The Indian peasant knows, however, not only how to take prompt advantage of a rise in prices, he knows also how to quickly recoup himself for the loss of a market. The re-extended cultivation in America led to a drop, eventually reaching to 30 millions sterling, in the Indian cotton exports. But the Indian peasant has more than made good the loss by the growth of other staples. The year 1865 was one of inflated markets throughout the world, and the Indian exports reached the unprecedented height of 69 millions. Last year, 1879–80, was a year of great depression in many markets, but the Indian exports again exceeded 69 millions sterling.

During the same period, vast numbers of people from the overcrowded interior of Bengal had been drafted off to the border districts, which, till the British obtained the country, were left waste through fear of the wild frontier races. These peasants, instead of starving in their old densely-populated homes, are now earning high wages on the tea plantations, and last year exported three millions sterling worth of tea.

All these are essentially rural industries, which owe

their existence to the new commercial life developed by the cities of British India. Besides such rural industries, however, there are a number of manufactures and productions which more especially appertain to the industrial life of great towns. Coal-mines have been discovered in several provinces, and now employ tens of thousands of miners. Mills and steam factories have followed the opening up of the coal-fields. Twenty-six years ago there was not a single loom worked by steam-power in India; there are now 1¼ million spindles employed in the cotton manufacture alone, and 40,000 spindles employed in the manufacture of jute.

Early in the last century, before the English became the ruling power in India, the country did not produce a million sterling a year of staples for exportation. During the first three-quarters of a century of our rule, the exports slowly rose to about eleven millions in 1830. During the half-century which has elapsed since that date, they have quickly multiplied by sixfold. In 1880, India sold to foreign nations 66 millions sterling worth of strictly Indian produce, which the Indian husbandman had reared, and for which he was paid. In that year, the total trade of India, including exports and imports, exceeded 122 millions sterling.

These figures are so great, and the material progress which they indicate is so enormous, that they elude the grasp of the imagination. It may assist us in realizing the change which they imply in the industrial life of the people to glance at the history of two single ports. I shall first take the local harbour of a rural district, Akyab, in British Burma. In 1826, when we obtained the province in which it is situated, Akyab was merely a fishing village. Within four years, by 1830, it had developed into a little town, with a trade valued at £7000. In 1879, the trade exceeded 2 millions sterling, so that the trade of Akyab has multiplied close on three hundredfold in fifty years. The other example is one on a larger scale. When we obtained Calcutta in 1686, it consisted of three mud hamlets, scarcely raised above the river slime, without any trade whatsoever. After a century and a half of British rule, the total value of the sea-borne trade of Calcutta in 1820 was 12 millions sterling. In 1879, it had risen to over 61¼ millions sterling, besides 45 millions of trade with the interior, making a total commerce of 106 millions sterling a year at a town which had not ten pounds' worth of external trade when the British settled there.

India has more to sell to the world than she requires to buy from it. During the five years ending 1879, the staples which she exported exceeded by an annual average of 21 millions sterling the merchandise which she imported. One-third of this balance she receives in cash; and during the five years she accumulated silver and gold, exclusive of re-exports, at the rate of 7 millions per annum. With another third, she pays interest at low rates for the capital with which she has constructed the material framework of her industrial life,—her railways (120 millions), irrigation works, cotton mills, coal-mines, indigo factories, tea-gardens, docks, steam-navigation lines, and debt. For that capital, she goes into the cheapest market in the world, London, and she remits the interest, not in cash, but in her own staples, which that capital has enabled her to produce and to bring to the sea-board. With the remaining third of her surplus exports, she pays the home charges of the Government to which she owes the peace and security that alone have rendered possible her industrial development. The home charges include not only the salaries of the supervising staff in England, and the pensions of the whole military and civil services, who have given their life's work to India, but the munitions of war, a section of the army, including the cost of its recruitment and transport, all stores for public works, and the whole *materiel* of a civilised administration. That *materiel* can be bought more cheaply in England than in India, and India's expenditure on good government is as essential an item for her industrial development, and repays her as high a profit, as the interest which she pays in England for the capital with which she has constructed her dockyards and railways. To sum up, India sells 21 millions a year more of her staples to foreign nations than the merchandise which she buys from them. She takes payment of one-third of the balance, or say 7 millions, in good government, and so secures that protection to person and property which she never had before, and which alone have rendered her industrial development possible. With another third, or 7 millions, she pays for the capital with which she has constructed the material framework of that development—pays for it at the lowest interest, and pays for it, not in cash, but in her own products. The remaining 7 millions she receives in gold and silver, and puts them in her purse.

I feel that I have taxed, perhaps too heavily, the reader's attention with so many figures. But it is impossible for any one to realize the progress made by India under British rule without having the statistics placed before him. Commerce and manufactures have been created for the people, vast outlets opened up for the productions of the country. The reader will perhaps pardon me for having wearied him with statistics when he remembers that those statistics mean a new industrial life for India—an industrial life which supersedes the sword of the invader and wholesale starvation by famine, in maintaining the balance between a population of small cultivators and the available land.

The effects of this new industrial life are not, however, confined to the great Indian cities. The new outlets for Indian staples have led to a rise in the price of the husbandman's crops, and in the value of the land on which they are grown. In many districts, during the last century, the entire price of a field was the value of the crop upon it. In fertile deltas the price of land did not exceed two years' purchase. In the same districts it is now from twelve to twenty years' purchase. It has been my duty to make inquiries in every province of India as to the interest which money yields. I find that for small loans to the cultivators, the old native rate of 37½ per cent. per annum still prevails. But if any one has a landed property to pledge, he can borrow at less than one-third of that rate of interest; and a native merchant of Calcutta who wishes to retire and purchase an estate, thinks himself fortunate if he can invest in land yielding 7 per cent. clear per annum. Landed property, which in the last century was one of the most precarious possessions, has now become the most secure form of investment in India, precisely as it is in England. The growth of rural rights, and the increase in the value of land, have advanced side by side with the creation of a new industrial life, and with the opening up of fresh outlets for the productions of the country.

These are a few of the results of English rule on the material development of India. It is not necessary for me here to dwell on the more obvious and often-recited aspects of that progress, on the network of roads and railways which we have spread over India, on the canals by which we have multiplied and secured her internal resources, or on the spacious harbours by which we have brought those resources into the market of the world. All these and many other agencies of material progress are involved in the one great fact, the creation of that new industrial life which has taken place under British rule. But, before closing this chapter, I should like to direct attention to a few of the moral aspects of that rule.

In the last century, education in India was a monopoly in the hands of the priests,—a power which they employed to subjugate the minds of the people. Under British rule, education in India has been taken entirely out of the hands of the priests, and it has become the great emancipator of the Indian races. In ancient India a Brahman was forbidden, on pain of death, to teach the sacred books to the masses. Under British rule, the State schools offer instruction to every one, and open the same careers to all. In the last century the Hindus were taught, from their earliest childhood, that they must remain imprisoned for life in the caste in which they were born. We have now two millions of boys and girls receiving public instruction in India. These two millions of native children are learning that every occupation and every profession in British India is open to every boy on the benches of an Indian school. The rising generation in India have been freed from superstitious terrors, they have been led to give up cruel practices, they have learned to detest and despise their forefathers' bloody rites. Widow-burning, infanticide, hook-swinging, self-mutilation, and human sacrifice,—these are a few familiar relics of the old bondage under which the Indian intellect cowered and the Indian heart bled. Great as has been the material progress of India during the past century, its emancipation from ignorance and priestcraft forms, to my mind, a far more splendid memorial of British rule. Truly the people that walked in darkness have seen a great light.

The result has been a revival of letters such as the world has never seen. On the 31st March 1818, the Serampur missionaries issued the first newspaper ever printed in a native language of India. The vernacular journals now exceed 230 in number, and are devoured every week by half a million readers. In 1878, 5000 books were published in India, besides a vast importation of literature from England. Of this mass of printed matter, only 500 were translations, the remaining 4500 being original works. The Indian intellect is marching forth in many directions, rejoicing in its new strength. More copies of books of poetry, philosophy, law, and religion issue every year from the press of British India than the whole manuscripts compiled during any century of native rule. In music, the revival has been effected on the old Sanskrit basis. One of my native friends has published a series of volumes on Indian music in English and Sanskrit; organized an orchestra of about 50 performers to illustrate the art; and presented complete collections of Hindu instruments to the Conservatoire at Paris, and other institutions in Europe. Among the earliest subjects which the new movement took as its theme, was the celebration of the Queen of England and her ancestors, in a Sanskrit volume entitled the *Victoria Gitika.*

The drama has in all ages been a great educator of the Indian races; and it was the first branch of Hindu literature to heartily accept the spoken dialects. The native theatre forms the best, indeed the only school in which an Englishman can acquaint himself with the indoor life of the people. He suddenly finds himself in an era of intense dramatic productiveness. Last year, 175 plays were published in India, and patriotic young natives form themselves into companies to produce their national dramas. Many of the pieces are vernacular renderings of stories from the Sanskrit epics. Others have a political significance, and deal with the phases of development upon which India has entered under the influence of British rule. One Bengali play, the *Nil-darpan*, or the Indigo Factory, became the subject of a celebrated trial in Calcutta; while others, such as *Ekei ki bale Sabhyata*, 'Is this what you call civilisation?' suggest serious thoughts to a candid English mind.

I have often been asked how it is that amidst this dayspring of the Indian intellect, Christianity makes so little way. The Hindus are one of the religious races of the earth. A series of great reformations during the past ten centuries have given to their national faith a vitality which has defied alike the persecutions and the persuasions of their conquerors. Last year, there were published in India 2 books of travels, 7 on politics, and 1502 on religion, or nearly a third of the whole works which issued from the press. Every great Indian reformer, from Buddha downwards, has, in spite of himself, had miraculous powers ascribed to him by the loving piety of his followers. At this moment, there is an able and earnest man walking about Calcutta, who, if his disciples can only refrain from writing his life for fifty years, will attain the dignity of a Divine Founder. Great tidal waves of religion are sweeping over the Indian mind. The theistic element in Hinduism has powerfully re-asserted itself as the Brahmo Samáj, or Deist Church of Bengal. The old Hindu dissenters, such as the Vaishnavs, have greatly increased their following, and new popular sects are springing up. Even orthodox Hinduism has financially prospered, the railways having done much to render pilgrimage pleasant. A century ago, Muhammadanism seemed to be dying of inanition in Bengal. In the mosques, or amid the serene palace life of the Musalmán nobility, a few *maulvis* of piety and learning calmly carried on the routine of their faith. But the Musalmán peasantry of Bengal had relapsed into a mongrel breed of circumcised Hindus, not one in ten of whom could recite the *kalma*—a simple creed, whose constant repetition is a matter of unconscious habit with all good Muhammadans. Under our rule, fervid Muhammadan missionaries have wandered from district to district, commanding the people to return to the pure faith, and denouncing God's wrath on the indifferent. A great body of the Bengali Musalmáns have purged themselves of rural superstitions, and evinced such an ardour of revivalist zeal as occasionally to cause some little inconvenience to the Government.

It is, therefore, not from any lack of the religious instinct in India, that Christianity fails to make progress. The Muhammadan ideal of a missionary is a lean old man with a staff and a couple of ragged disciples. Among the Hindus, for the past 2400 years, every preacher who would appeal to the popular heart must fulfil two conditions, and conform to a certain type,—he must cut himself off from the world by a solemn act, like the Great Renunciation of Buddha; and he must come forth from his solitary self-communings with a simple message. This message need not be original, for it must consist of a re-assertion, in some form, of the unity of God and the equality of man. One poor low-caste, who issued, haggard and naked, from the jungles of the Central Provinces, with only a broken cry of 'Sat-nám, Sat-nám, Sat-nám,' 'The True God, the True God, the True God,' and a message not to drink spirits, made over a quarter of a million of followers before his death in 1850.

Our missionaries do not seem to the natives to belong to this type. They are highly regarded as men of letters and as teachers of youth, as the guides who first opened up the stores of western knowledge to India, and who are still the pioneers of education among the backward races. The mission printing-presses may be said to have created Bengali as a literary language, and to have developed ruder tongues, like Santáli and Assamese, into written vehicles for thought. But, whatever may be the self-sacrifices of our missionaries, or the internal conflicts which they endure, their lives do not appear to the poor toilers of the rice-field in the light of a Great Renunciation. To the natives, the missionary seems to be a charitable Englishman who keeps an excellent cheap school, speaks the language well, preaches a European form of their old incarnations, and drives out his wife and little ones in a pony-carriage. This friendly neighbour, this affectionate husband, this good man, is of an estimable type, of a type which has done much to raise the English character in the eyes of the natives, but not of the traditional type to which the popular preacher in India must conform.

The missionary has neither the personal sanctity nor

the simple message of the visionary who comes forth from his fastings and temptation in the forest. Instead, he has a dogmatic theology which, when he discusses it with the Brahmans, seems to the unprepared populace to resolve itself into a wrangle as to the comparative merits of the Hindu triad and the European Trinity, and the comparative evidence for the incarnation of Krishna and the incarnation of Christ. The uneducated native prefers, if he is to have a triad and an incarnation, to keep his own ones. The educated native thinks that triads and incarnations belong to a stage of mental development which he has passed.

It should be remembered, however, that apart from the higher claims of Christianity, there are always a number of human chances running in its favour in India. Its propaganda is supported by a steady supply of capital which none of the native proselytizing sects can command. It maintains, therefore, a continuity of effort and a constant exertion of brain-power which the intenser but more spasmodic apostles of other creeds cannot rival. There is the possibility, any day, of some missionary striking the native imagination as a religious reformer of the true Indian type, and converting half a million of people. The Christian missions are, moreover, great educational agencies, and naturally attract to their faith a certain number of the young minds which they train and develop. The dearths which periodically afflict the country also tend to swell the Christian population, as the missionaries are often the best available guardians to whom the State can make over the thousands of orphans that a great famine leaves behind. The schisms among the Hindu theistic sects may from time to time lead wearied inquirers after truth to seek rest within the authoritative Christian dogma. Already the Christian population numbers 1½ millions; over one million being Roman Catholics, and under half a million Protestants. While, therefore, Christianity has to contend with fundamental difficulties in India, it has, merely from the human point of view, many permanent chances in its favour. No one who has studied the facts would venture to predict that it may not, some day, strike root as one of the popular religions of India.

Meanwhile the intellectual upheaval is profoundly influencing family life. European ideas are knocking at the door of the zanána, and we hear confused cries from within, which seem to show that the death-like monotony of woman's existence in India is broken. The degradation of the female intelligence means the loss of one-half its brain-power to a nation. Last October, while I was writing these pages, an accomplished Brahman lady was travelling through Bengal with her brother, holding public meetings on the education and emancipation of women. 'They were received everywhere,' says an Indian correspondent, 'with great enthusiasm by the Hindus, who were delighted to hear their holy Sanskrit from a woman's lips. It seemed to them as if Saraswatí (the goddess of Eloquence) had come down to visit them. Instead of a hot, confined room, we had a long and broad terrace, open to the sky, and with the Ganges flowing at our feet. The meeting was at half-past four in the afternoon, by which time the terrace was shaded from the sun by trees and houses to the westward. At the eastern end of the terrace, a small marble table, with a glass of flowers on it, and some chairs were set, and there Roma stood up, facing the west, and addressed her audience. On her right was the Ganges, covered with large broad-sailed boats of a type which has perhaps lasted for 2000 years. There was little or nothing around to remind her or her audience of European civilisation. The clear blue sky and the broad river coming sweeping down from the walls of Benares dominated everything else. It was such a place as Buddha might have chosen for addressing his followers.'

This young lady is twenty-two years of age, the daughter of a learned *pandit* and public official, slight and girlish-looking, with a fair complexion and light grey eyes. She is now engaged to be married to a Bengali pleader, an M.A. of the Calcutta University.

Side by side with the stirring of the Indian intellect there has also been an awakening of the Indian races to a new political life. The old village communities of India, with their rural guilds and castes, and all the good and evil which they implied, had in many provinces lost their vitality before the commencement of the English rule. Their memories and their outward forms survived; but the life had been trodden out of them beneath the heel of the Musalmán taxgatherer and the hoofs of the Marhatta cavalry. In some parts the village institutions had ceased to protect the peasantry from external oppression, or even to settle their disputes among themselves. Every attempt on a large-scale to resuscitate the ancient village community has failed. For a time the English rulers were content to deplore this fact—a fact which, in reality, marks the advance of a race from a lower to a higher stage of social organization. But during the past twenty-five years efforts have been made to develop a new political life in place of the old village guilds which had disappeared. The village has given place to the municipality in India. Before our own eyes we see the self-government, which the primitive village communities had ceased to give, developing into a higher form of self-government under municipal institutions. At this moment there are nearly one thousand municipalities in India, with a municipal population exceeding fourteen millions, and raising among themselves for local purposes a revenue of close on two millions sterling. There are also, in some of the provinces, district boards and rural unions, which do for the country what the municipalities do for the towns. The Indian races are visibly passing from the village into the municipal stage of social organization; and the first lessons in local government are being learned by fourteen millions of native citizens.

THE WORK TO BE DONE.

III. THE ADJUSTMENT OF THE FOOD SUPPLY TO THE GROWING POPULATION.

THERE is, as I mentioned at starting, another side to the picture. Good work has been done by our countrymen in India, but greater difficulties now confront them. The population has in many parts outgrown the food-producing powers of the soil. To some observers the situation seems so hopeless, that a magazine writer lately urged that we should retire from a spectacle of overcrowded human misery which we are powerless to relieve. But the English are not a people to take on themselves a great national task like the government of India, and then to desert the ship when the breakers come in sight. To others, the cause for despair is that the difficulty proceeds from the very merits of our rule; and that the better we do our duty by India, the more the people will multiply, and the harder will become their struggle for life. To despondents of this nobler class, I would say, 'Look back at what our countrymen have already achieved in India, and you will not despair of what they may yet accomplish.' Their history from the commencement has been a narrative of great difficulties overcome. A hundred years ago no one would have ventured to predict the united peaceful India of the present day. Therefore it is that I have tried to show what British rule has done in India, in order that we may, with a firm heart, examine what it has yet to do for the Indian people.

I shall now ask attention to two of the saddest problems with which a State can be called to deal—namely, the poverty of the people, and the alleged inability of the Government to pay its way. With these fundamental problems yet unsolved in India, it may seem a delusive optimism to speak of the success of the British administration. It profits little that we have put an end to invasion from without, established order and security in place of anarchy and rapine within, covered the land with schools and court-houses, with roads, railways, and canals, and given a vast impulse to population and trade,—all this profits little if the people have not enough to eat, and if the country cannot support the cost of our rule. There is some exaggeration, but there is also much truth in criticism such as this. The poverty of a densely-crowded population of small cultivators, and the difficulty of defraying a civilised government from the revenues of an Asiatic country, lie at the very root of our position in India. These are the initial facts with which we have to struggle, and until they are accepted as the basis of this country's dealings with India, our financial position there will be one of danger.

India was for long in the unfortunate position of a

man who is supposed to be richer than he really is. If the British nation had realized the poverty of India, it would have refrained from several acts which now form standing reproaches against England in the native press. Fortunately for the national honour, the list of our injustices to India, although sufficiently painful to all who wish to see this country discharge its great duties in a noble spirit, is not a very long one. But under pressure of party exigencies and class interests in England, that list may at any moment be added to. For example, we should think it passing strange if we were taxed in London in order to set up an English museum in Calcutta. Yet a proposal was not long ago made to charge, at least in part, to the Indian revenues, the cost of an Indian museum in London. I am glad to say that this attempt failed. Indeed, it has ended in the Indian exhibitions in London being henceforth maintained at the expense of the nation which enjoys them, and in a saving (I am told) of £15,000 a year formerly charged to the Indian revenues. When next you visit the Amravati sculptures at the British Museum, or the gorgeous Indian rooms and their delicate art products at South Kensington, you may have the satisfaction of knowing that your pleasure is honestly paid for by the English Exchequer.

I hope that this country will realize once and for all the poverty of the people from whom the Indian revenues are raised. When we have clearly recognised this, we shall see that the smallest act of financial sharp-dealing with India is an act not only of iniquity but of cruelty and meanness, and one which carries with it lasting reproach.

How comes it that India was once held to be so rich, and now proves to be so poor? The wealth of the East Indies was handed down as a tradition from Roman times, and has for centuries been an accepted belief in Europe. There is usually an element of truth in such a belief, and the traditional wealth of India appeared to rest on a very solid basis. In the first place, India has always been the greatest accumulator of the precious metals known to commerce. Besides her own production of gold, by no means inconsiderable in ancient times, and perhaps destined to be again revived on a great scale in our own day, India absorbed bullion to an extent which seemed, to the economists of bygone centuries, to threaten the depletion of Europe. But if the power of amassing gold and silver be accepted as a proof of the wealth of a country, India is richer now than ever. Roman patriots deplored that the eastern trade, including China, India, and Arabia, drained the empire of three-quarters of a million sterling of silver per annum; and the loudest complaint against the East India Company in the seventeenth century was aimed at its privilege—a privilege guarded by many restrictions—of exporting £30,000 a year of bullion and foreign coin to the East. Well, the average importation of gold and silver into India during the past ten years averaged 9 millions sterling per annum; and in 1878 it exceeded 17 millions. Of this enormous sum, India retains by far the greatest proportion. Thus, after deducting all re-exports, so far as they can be ascertained, by sea, India accumulated close on seventy millions sterling in gold and silver during the past ten years.

There is another sense in which India appeared to our ancestors to be a very wealthy country. It contained a number of kings and princes, and the lavish magnificence alike of the Imperial and of the local courts seemed a proof of the inexhaustible riches of the people. The early travellers never realized that India was the size of all Europe less Russia, and that the Indian courts must be compared in number and display, not with the palace of his own single sovereign at home, but with all the courts of Europe. The Indian princes, moreover, were compelled by the absence of any system of national credit, to hoard great sums with a view to meeting sudden demands, such as the mutiny of their troops or the rebellion of a too powerful kinsman. These hoards they kept to a large extent in precious gems, so that the national reserve fund was also a principal means of courtly display. When Nadír Sháh sacked Delhi in 1739, and cleared out the Imperial treasures, he found, if we may believe our authorities, 3½ millions of specie, and 28½ millions worth of jewels, ornaments, and plate. Of the specie, only one million is said—I know not on what original evidence—to have been in gold or silver coin. From the treasury of Bengal, the richest province of the empire, our countrymen in 1757 extracted about 1½ millions sterling, but only £58,000 in rupees, the rest being in specie and jewels. The cash balances of the British Government of India varied between 1870 and 1878 from 25 to 15 millions sterling. But the British cash balances are hidden away in strong rooms out of sight; while the Peacock Throne blazed with its diamonds before the eyes of every foreign ambassador.

There is more accumulated wealth held by natives in two cities of British India, Calcutta and Bombay,—cities which a couple of centuries ago were mud-hut hamlets,—than all the treasures of the Imperial and local courts under the Mughal Empire. The magnificence of the rich natives still excites the admiration of European travellers. In a narrative of a recent Indian journey, the President of the Cheshire Salt Chamber of Commerce dwells on the costly entertainments given by native residents of Calcutta to over a thousand guests. 'Gentlemen at home,' he says, 'who repeat the cant phrase "the poverty of India," should witness a scene like this, and we warrant they would be cured. Our host, a man still in the full prime of life, is the architect of his own great fortune, gained in lawful commerce. The expenditure of ten thousand pounds upon one entertainment by a private citizen does not smack much of the poverty of the country.' If, therefore, we are content to accept travellers' tales of the magnificence of native grandees as a proof of the wealth of the country, India's old reputation for riches might stand as high as ever.

But we cannot accept such proof. We judge nowadays of the wealth of nations not by the splendour of individuals, but by the prosperity of the people. This test the early European travellers never applied to India. If they had applied it, they would have found that beneath the extravagance of the few lay the misery of the many. Their own narratives supply evidence that the common lot in India was a very wretched one under the native dynasties; and a hundred years of British rule have scarcely sufficed to obliterate the traces of oppression and rural servitude which those dynasties left behind. The change in our views regarding the wealth or poverty of India results from the application of the more enlightened tests, by which political economy has taught us to judge of the well-being of a people.

Judged by those standards, India is, and ever since it came under modern observation has always been, a poor country. Alike under Mughal and British rule, we see a population of small husbandmen contending, without any reserve of capital, against the chances and misfortunes of the tropical year. The lives of millions of families have depended each autumn on a few inches more or less of rainfall. The calamities inseparable from such a condition of things were intensified under native rule by invasions from without; by rebellions, feuds, and hordes of banditti within; and by the perpetual oppression of the weak by the strong. On the other hand, these disorders to some extent worked their own cure. They kept down the population, and the pressure of the people on the soil was much less severe than it now is. When India passed into our hands in the last century, there was plenty of good land for every one who wanted it. The importance of this fact to a people consisting entirely of cultivators can scarcely be over-rated. In 1789, the Governor-General declared, after three years' vigilant inquiry, that one-third of Bengal lay unoccupied. Only the best lands in the Province were cultivated; and the landholders, where they existed, had to treat their peasantry well; for the competition was among the proprietors for tenants, and not among the tenants for land.

Under such conditions, the means of existence were easily raised, and the people had only to be protected from plunder and the sword in order to prosper. The establishment of British rule afforded that protection almost from the first; and by degrees, as the English conscience awoke more fully to its responsibilities in India, it has endeavoured to combat the other two ancient devastators, namely, pestilence and famine. No sooner does one of the old epidemics break out in a district, than an army of doctors, native and European, marches forth to do battle with it; and the Government has set up as a great Cinchona planter, in order to bring the cheap quinine alkaloids within reach of the people. Something has also been done, although much more remains to be accomplished, to mitigate the periodical famines which were formerly accepted as inevitable concomitants of the climate. One by one the old checks on an Asiatic population have been removed. I have just mentioned that a century ago one-third of Bengal lay unoccupied; but since then, the population of Bengal has increased not by one-third, but threefold; and the area which had to feed 21 millions in 1780, has in 1880 to feed over 63 millions of mouths. After a minute comparison of rural India at present with the facts disclosed in the manuscript records, I am compelled to the conclusion, that throughout large tracts, the struggle for life is harder than it was when the country passed into our hands.

For not only have the British districts to support a much denser population than they had a century ago, but they have to feed a population nearly three times as dense as that in the Native States at the present day. Throughout all British India, the average population is 212 persons to the square mile; or deducting the comparatively new and outlying provinces of British Burma and Assam, it is 243 persons to the square mile. The average population in Native or Feudatory India is, so far as we can discover, 89 persons to the square mile. Excluding, therefore, Assam on the eastern frontier, and Burma beyond the sea, each square mile of British India has to feed on an average nearly three times as many mouths as each square mile of the Native States. How thick this population is, may be realized from the fact that fertile France has only 180 people to the square mile; while even in crowded England, where-ever the density approaches 200 to the square mile, it ceases to be a rural population, and has to live by manufactures, mines, or city industries.

We speak of the poverty and the miserably small farms of the Irish peasant. Well, Ireland has, according to the last census, 169 persons to the square mile. But we can take thirteen districts of Northern India, equal in size to Ireland, which have to support an average of 680 persons to the square mile, or over one person to each acre. This calculation, it must be remembered, allows no deduction for swamps, wastes, and land incapable of tillage. The Famine Commissioners report that two-thirds of the whole farmers of Bengal have holdings of between 2 and 3 acres. If we allow four persons to each peasant family, we find 24 millions of human beings struggling to live off the produce of 15 million acres, or just over half an acre apiece. The Indian soil cannot support that struggle.

We may object to sensational writing, but we cannot wonder that patriotic Englishmen who have never been in India, and who suddenly catch sight of the results of this state of things without a previous knowledge of the causes, should head their essays with such titles as 'Bleeding to Death.'

The above figures fail, indeed, to present the facts in their full significance. For Ireland, like the rest of Great Britain, has many cities and centres of manufacturing industry, while in India practically the whole people has to make its livelihood by the tillage of the land. Thus, in England and Wales, 42 per cent., or nearly one-half of the population, dwell, according to the last census, in towns with upwards of 20,000 inhabitants; while in British India, under 5 per cent., or not one-twentieth, dwell in such towns. Ninety per cent. of the rural population have to live more or less entirely by the tillage of the soil. India, therefore, is almost exclusively a country of peasant farmers, and many of the so-called towns are merely groups of villages, in the midst of which the ploughman drives his cattle a-field, and all the operations of agriculture go on. Indeed, the term municipality, which in Europe is only applied to towns, means quite as often in India a collection of rural homesteads for the purposes of local government.

The increasing population has driven from the open country the larger sorts of wild beasts. It is also exhausting the waters of their fishes. About 80 per cent. of the natives are permitted by their caste rules to eat this kind of food—practically the only animal food available to the Indian husbandman. The price of fish has doubled, and for a time the fishing castes prospered greatly. In time, however, the enormously increased consumption began to tell. The fishermen plied their trade harder, and contracted the meshes of their nets till not a minnow could pass through them. The fishes in India never have a day's rest—no close season is allowed for breeding time, and even the spawn is gathered for food. The young fry, which would grow into large fish, are sold by jars-full, about two hundred being required to make a pound. They are caught by every device of human ingenuity—by traps, nets, baskets, weirs, poisoning, suffocation by cloths, and draining off the water from the streams, marshes, and ponds. In 1871, returns collected from all India disclosed an alarming decrease in this most important source of food supply. Almost everywhere the yield had ceased to be equal to the demand. In some parts, the fishing castes had so exhausted the waters that many of them had to give up their hereditary trade and become tillers of the soil. In others, the people were eating frogs instead of fish, cooking them in the same way, and distinguishing between the comparative delicacy of the 'solitary,' 'green,' and 'spangled' species.

Another effect of the increased population is the growth of landless classes. The cultivated area no longer suffices to allow a plot of ground for every peasant, and vast multitudes now find themselves ousted from the soil. The census of 1872 returned 7½ million males in this category; or, allowing for women and children, about 24 millions. They earn a poor and precarious subsistence as hired labourers. Numbers of them go through their lives in a state of chronic hunger; they are the class whom a scarcity first attacks, and who supply the mass of the victims in a famine.

To the peasant farmer, the result of the increase in population is twofold: he gets a smaller return from the land for his labour, and he has to pay away a larger proportion of that smaller return to his landlord. For with the increase of population, the peasantry had to fall back on inferior or less favourably situated soils. The fact that a third of a province lay waste might be an unfortunate, or even a discreditable fact for the Government, but it did not necessarily involve any hardship to the tiller of the soil. Only the best lands in a village, and only the best villages in a district, were cultivated. The rest were entered in the accounts of the Native Administration as 'unoccupied.' As the people multiplied under our rule, they had to bring into tillage these inferior lands, and so by degrees they have had to expend a larger amount of labour in order to raise the same quantity of food. As the increase of the population went on, they could no longer allow the soil any rest, and many thousands of acres have to produce two crops each year. Moreover, the surrounding jungle was gradually ploughed up, and the people had to fall back upon the cow-dung for fuel. In this way both the two great sources of manure were cut off—namely, the ashes from the wood which they formerly burned, and the ammonia and other volatile parts of the cow-dung which they now burn in place of timber.

Many careful observers believe, indeed, that the clearing and cultivation of the jungles have been carried to such an excess in some parts of India as to seriously alter the climate. For forests, and the undergrowth which they foster, not only husband the rainfall, but they appear to attract it. A hill covered with forest is a reservoir of moisture; the same hill stripped of its woods becomes hard, arid ground, down whose bare surface the tropical rains rush off in destructive torrents, instead of sinking into the subsoil, or being stored up in the vegetation. It is alleged that the risk of drought and famine has increased in many parts of India from this cause; and whereas the great object of the ancient native dynasties was to get the cultivators to clear the jungle, the British Government finds a costly Department necessary to conserve the forests which still remain.

The pasture grounds of the villages have also, to a

large extent, been brought under the plough, and the cattle in many districts have degenerated from insufficient food. The same number of oxen can no longer put the same amount of work into the soil. Terrible outbreaks of the cow epidemic and the foot-and-mouth disease sweep across Bengal, and some years ago necessitated the appointment of a Cattle Plague Commission. While, therefore, the husbandman has now to wring a subsistence out of inferior lands which he would not have touched a hundred years ago, the good lands have deteriorated for want of manure and from want of rest, and the cattle have degenerated from lack of pasture. This sad description does not apply, as I shall presently show, to all India, but it represents the state of things in large and increasing areas where the population has outgrown the food-producing powers of the land. It explains, and to some extent justifies, the mournful forebodings of those who warn us that our real danger in India is not any temporary insolvency of the finances, but a permanent bankruptcy of the soil.

Of the smaller crops which the husbandman thus extracts from the soil, he has to give a larger share to the landlord; for rent represents, fundamentally, the difference in value between the most profitable and the least profitable lands under cultivation. This is the economical theory, and in spite of every effort at limitation by custom or law, the economical theory constantly tends to assert itself in the actual facts. As the peasantry in Bengal have been forced back upon the poorer lands, the natural rent of all the other lands has risen. A large and prosperous body of proprietors has grown up under our rule. Their prosperity has resulted partly from their own good management, but chiefly from the husbandmen having been forced by their growing numbers to bring into tillage the inferior lands, and from the natural increase of rent to which that process gives rise as regards the superior soils.

We may realize the revolution thus silently effected in the rural economy of India from two facts—a historical fact and a legal one. The historical fact, is that when the English obtained Bengal in the last century, they found two classes of tenants—the *thâni* or 'stationary' husbandman, with occupancy rights in the soil, and the *pâikâsht* or floating rural population, without such rights. At that time, so great was the surplus of land, that the proprietors were glad to attract the floating population to their estates by giving them farms at lower rates than those paid by the stationary tenants. The latter had built their own homesteads, dug wells or tanks, and would submit to a higher rent rather than abandon their holdings, and lose the capital and labour invested in them. It thus resulted that rack-rents, that is to say, the rents paid by tenants without leases or occupancy rights, were, in parts of Bengal, lower than the rents paid by tenants with occupancy rights. This state of things is now reversed. The ever-increasing rack-rents exacted by the landlords from the tenants without leases or occupancy rights form the great complaint of the rural population, and one of the most difficult problems with which the Government has to deal.

The legal fact is that the enhancement of rent, which never came within the contemplation of the law-makers of the last century in Bengal, is now the vital question of legislation. Our first attempt to ascertain and define the land law of Bengal is embodied in the Cornwallis Code of 1793. The difficulty at that time was where to get tenants, not how to raise their rent. Enhancement finds no mention in the Code. So far as can be inferred from the spirit of its provisions, the Indian Legislature seems to have assumed that the proprietors were thenceforward to pay the same land-tax for ever to the Government, and that the tenants were thenceforward to pay the same rates of rent for ever to the proprietors. But before the middle of the present century, rents had been enhanced to such a degree as to threaten an agrarian dead-lock. It was found absolutely necessary to revise the land law; and 1859, the year after the country passed under the Crown, is memorable in Bengal for the second great Land Code. Restraints upon the enhancement of rents form the most important features of this Land Code of 1859. But in spite of its provisions, the increase of the people and the natural operation of economic laws have led to a still further rise in rent. The peasantry resisted by every legal means, and in some parts combined to ruin the landlords by refusing to pay rent. Their attitude was in certain respects similar to the position of the Irish peasantry. The Indian husbandman has, however, a power of pacific combination, and of patient, passive resistance, which the Irish cotters have not yet developed. The most peaceful district of Bengal, Pabna, was for some time in a state of agrarian revolt. But it was a revolt conducted, as a rule, according to the strict forms of law. With the exception of a few quite insignificant ebullitions, the husbandmen simply said: 'We shall not fight, but we shall not pay. We shall claim occupancy rights; and every single rent which you landlords collect shall cost you a law-suit. This we shall contest at each stage, from the institution of the plaint to the final order for selling us up, by every delay, appeal, and other weapon of chicanery known to the law. You will get your decree in the long-run; but in the meantime you will be ruined. For ourselves, we are as badly off as we can be, and it is better for us to sell our last cow to fight you in the courts than to pay your rent with it.' In Bengal, 6 millions, or two-thirds of the whole tenantry, pay rents of less than ten shillings a year. Among such a nation of small cultivators, it is simply impossible to collect every petty rent by a law-suit, and their combination really did mean ruin to many of the landlords. The Government, while it declared that it would maintain public order, counselled private concessions. Some sort of compromise was arrived at, and the Legislature obtained a breathing-space to again consider the whole questions involved. The result is a new Land Code, the draft of which has just reached England. In this Code, the most prominent question is again the enhancement of rent, and its provisions are more stringent than ever in favour of the tenant.

'Where the subdivision of land among tenants-at-will is extreme,' write the Famine Commissioners in 1880, 'and in a country where agriculture is almost the only possible employment for large classes of the people, the competition is so keen that rents can be forced up to a ruinous height, and men will crowd each other till the space left to each is barely sufficient to support a family.' If they relax their grasp on their holding, they sink into the landless classes.

Such is the state of things in Bengal, where landlordism and great proprietors chiefly prevail. But in other parts of India, the British Government has retained the land in its own hands, as it was kept by the previous native dynasties, and deals directly with the cultivators. The Government is the landlord itself, and it is necessary to see how it has behaved to its tenants. Bengal forms the most typical representative of the former system, and Madras is usually taken as the most typical representative of the latter. But even in Madras, the British rulers have made over a large part of their territory (paying about one-eighth of the land revenue), to private proprietors; and my remarks will be confined to the remaining seven-eighths, which remain in the hands of the Government. The population has here also increased, and the people have been forced back upon inferior soils. The figures have been worked out only for the past quarter of a century, that is, from 1853 to 1878. They show the following results.

In 1853, the general population was estimated at 22 millions; in 1878, at 31½ millions, showing an increase of 43 per cent., or nearly one-half. The cultivated land, held by husbandmen direct from the State, had increased from 12 to 20 millions of acres, or 66 per cent., exactly two-thirds. The area of tillage had, therefore, not only kept pace with the increase of population, but had extended at a rate of 50 per cent. more rapidly. This resulted partly from the fact that the inferior lands, now reclaimed, could not support so large an average of people as the superior lands which were already in cultivation at the commencement of the period. The Government recognised this, and has accordingly increased its rental only from 3 millions to 3⅘ millions sterling; being only 26 per cent., or one-fourth, while the area of cultivation has increased by 66 per cent. The Government, in fact, has reduced its average rental over the total area of cultivation from 5s. an acre in 1853 to 3s. 10d. an acre in 1878, or over 23 per cent., say one-fourth. According to the ordinary theory of rent, rates should have risen enormously during that period; and they have risen enormously wherever the land is held by private proprietors. As regards the Madras Presidency, therefore, the facts may be recapitulated thus. During the 25 years the area of cultivation has increased by 66 per cent., or two-thirds; the population by 43 per cent., or nearly one-half; and the Government rental by only 26 per cent., or one-fourth; while the average rates of rent per acre have been actually reduced by over 23 per cent., or nearly one-fourth, from

5s. an acre in 1853 to 3s. 10d. an acre in 1878. Instead of taking advantage of the increase of population to enhance the rental, the Madras Government has realized the fact that the increase in numbers means a harder struggle for life, and has reduced instead of enhancing, according to the economic laws of rent, the average rates throughout its domains.

But a crowded population of small cultivators, without capital, and with no restraints on marriage, everywhere is, has been, and must be, poor. Remember that each Hindu marries as a religious duty, and that marriage takes place at the close of childhood, quite irrespective of there being any means of subsistence for the young couple. That is the root of the evil. In districts where the soil is poor, or the rainfall uncertain, the people have always had to depend upon village money-lenders for the capital necessary to feed them till the next harvest. Amid the tumults of native rule, the usurers lent comparatively small sums. If the peasant failed to pay, they could not evict him or sell his holding; because, among other reasons, there was more land than there were people to till it. The native Government, moreover, could not afford to lose a tenant. Accordingly the bankrupt peasant went on, year after year, paying as much interest as the money-lender could squeeze out of him; until the next Marhattá invasion or Muhammadan rebellion swept away the whole generation of usurers, and so cleared up the account. Under our rule there is no chance of such relief for insolvent debtors; and our rigid enforcement of contracts, together with the increase of the population, has armed the creditor with powers formerly unknown. For the peasant's holding under the British Government has become a valuable property, and he can be readily sold out, as there are always plenty of husbandmen anxious to buy in. The result is twofold. In the first place, the village banker lends larger sums, for the security is increased; and in the second place, he can push the peasantry to extremities by eviction, which was economically impossible under native rule.

In certain districts of Southern India, the people are sometimes driven by misery to take the law into their own hands. They kill the village usurer, or burn down his house with his account-books, and perhaps himself in it. But this offence, which was a common and venial one under native rule, now brings upon the perpetrators the inflexible arm of the British law. Of late years there has been an agrarian agitation in Southern India, similar in some respects to the agrarian agitation in Bengal. But in the south, where the Government as proprietor has granted peasant tenures, the revolt has been against the usurers, while in Bengal it has been against the landlords. In Southern India the demand is for legislative restraints on selling out the husbandman for debt; in Bengal it is for legislative restraints on the enhancement of his rent.

The sad result seems to be, that whether we give over the land to a proprietary class, as in Bengal, or keep it in our own hands, as in Southern India, the struggle for life grows harder to large sections of the people. But those sections, although numbered by millions, fortunately do not make up the whole population. Throughout wide tracts where land is still plentiful, the peace and security of British rule produce a permanent prosperity never before reached in India. I have tried to look with my own eyes into the condition of the tillers of the soil in almost every country of Europe, from Norway to the Black Sea, but I know of no peasantry so well off as the husbandmen in Eastern Bengal and many other parts of India. Vast trading classes have also been developed under our Government, who enjoy a degree of comfort which no considerable body of the people possessed when the country passed into our hands. But the comfortable classes, whether husbandmen or traders, keep silence. The uncomfortable classes very properly make themselves heard.

You now know what I mean by the poverty of the Indian people. More food is raised from the land than ever was raised before; but the population has increased at even a more rapid rate than the food-supply. We are compelled to stand by and watch the pitiless operation of economic laws, whose force no man can stay. Those laws decree that a population of small husbandmen which marries and multiplies irrespective of the means of subsistence, shall suffer a constantly increasing struggle for existence. But while it is important to clearly realize this evil, it is necessary to calmly gauge its proportions. Nothing is more dangerous to a government than ignorance, and few things are so terrifying as half-knowledge. However great may be the pressure upon certain classes of the people, India produces each harvest more food than she consumes. She exported during the last five years an average of over 23 million cwts. of food-grains alone, capable of feeding her whole population for ten days, or an additional 5½ millions of people for the entire year. This makes no allowance for the other edible seeds, oils, and condiments which she exports. We may put it in another way. During the past five years, India has sold an average of under 8 millions worth of food-grains to other nations. This sum is rather more than equal to the balance of over 7 millions sterling which she receives in cash for her exports; after paying for all her imports, for the interest on money raised in England, and for all the home charges of the Government. With these 8 millions sterling she could, if she pleased, pay for another 23 million cwts. of food. In either case, we find that the Indian harvest produces a surplus equal to the whole consumpt of her population during ten days, or to the support of an extra 5½ millions of people during an entire year.

It may, however, be alleged with some truth, that if the whole population ate as much as they could, this surplus would not exist. The grain exports of India represent many hungry stomachs in India. On the one hand, it is incorrect to say that those exports of food are compulsory in order to pay for the English charges of the Government. For the value of the whole food exports of India only slightly exceeds the 7 millions sterling which she yearly hoards in gold and silver, after paying for her imports, for interest on English capital, and for all home charges of the Government. Those expenses would be defrayed by her other exports, even if she did not send out a bag of grain from her harbours. On the other hand, if all the poorer classes in India ate two full meals every day, the surplus for export would be much less than at present. That surplus only proves that the yearly supply of food in India is greater than the effective demand for it.

There is, however, another way of approaching the question. I have taken all the provinces for which returns exist, and endeavoured to find out what amount of food they yield per head of the population. Our experience in famines shows that 1¼ lbs. of grain a day, or say 450 lbs. per annum, will keep a working adult male in health. That allowance becomes a comfortable one if granted for a whole population of men, women, and children; supplemented as it is in the Indian homesteads, by milk, oils, condiments, fruits, vegetables, and occasionally fish. From the statement on the next page, it will be seen that in every province for which returns exist, the average produce of the local crops is over 600 lbs. per person, while 450 lbs. is the average required to maintain the people in health. That table does not include the acreage under other crops, which go to pay the rent. Even Burma, where the peasantry have enough and to spare, only consumes 507 lbs. per head. According to the Famine Commissioners, Burma raises a total of 1½ million tons, or 1087 lbs. per head. But, deducting exports, etc., she only consumes for ordinary purposes, 700,000 tons, or 507 lbs. per head. This shows

An Attempt to show the Food-Supply of British India.

Province.	Population.	Total Area in Sq. Miles.	Cultivated Area in Sq. Miles.	Cultivable Waste.	Uncultivable and Balance.	Area under Food Crops, in Million Acres.	Total Produce of Food, in Million Tons.	Produce of Food per Acre, in lbs.	Pressure of Pop. on whole Land, per Sq. Mile.	Pressure of Pop. on Cultivated Land, per Sq. Mile.	Annual Food-Supply per Person, in lbs.
I.	II.	III.	IV.	V.	VI.	VII.	VIII.	IX.	X.	XI.	XII.
*	*	*	†	†	†	‡	‡	‡	*	‖	¶
Bengal, . .	60,738,217	156,286	85,000	No returns.	No returns.	48·5	17·20	806	388	715	634
Assam, . .	4,124,972	45,303	7,500	18,000?	19,803	No returns.			91	550	No returns.
N.W. Provinces, .	30,781,204	81,778 }	51,000	19,600	35,391	31	11·25	813	376 }	824	602
Oudh, . . .	11,224,095	24,213 }							463 }		
Punjab, . .	17,611,498	107,010	35,000	30,000	42,010	18·5	5·25	635	163	503	611
Central Provinces, ϕ	9,223,534	113,320 ϕ	30,000	40,000	43,320	13	2·75	470	83	307	667
Berar, . . .	2,227,654	17,711	10,156	No returns.	No returns.	3·75	·62	369	126	220	621
Mysore, . .	5,055,412	29,633	8,600	No returns.	No returns.	5	1·50	672	170	588	664
British Burma, .	3,088,902	87,464	5,000	37,000	45,464	2·70	1·50	1244	35	617	1087
Madras, . .	31,385,820	138,856	50,000	No returns.	No returns.	29	8·50	658	228	627	607
Bombay (parts of), **	...	50,000	30,000	8,000	12,000	19·25	3·80	415	132	...	...

* Cols. I., II., III., and X. are reproduced from Statement No. 1., Statistical Abstract relating to British India, presented to Parliament 14th Nov. 1880.

† Cols. IV. and V. are taken from the Report of the Indian Famine Commission, Part ii. pp. 75-77: Col. VI. gives the balance between them and Col. III.

‡ Cols. VII., VIII., and IX. are taken from the Famine Commission Report, Part ii. pp. 71-75. For various reasons, Col. IX. will not work out exactly from Cols. VII. and VIII., and is simply reproduced from the F. C. Report.

‖ Col. XI. is worked from Cols. II. and IV.

¶ Col. XII. is worked from Cols. II. and VIII.

ϕ The figures for the Central Provinces include the Native States attached to them.

** I have returns for only 50,000 square miles, out of the total of 124,105 square miles in the Presidency of Bombay, with Sind. Nor are any returns available for Ajmere—area, 2711 square miles; population, 396,889; or for Coorg—area, 1572 square miles; population, 168,312. Total excluded British area, about 78,000 square miles; population, about 7 millions. On the other hand, 29,112 square miles, and a population of 1,049,710, are included under the Central Provinces for the attached Native States.

that one of the best-fed provinces in the world, where there is still more land than there are husbandmen to till it, and abundance of fish, cannot consume much more grain than the rate I have allowed of 450 lbs. per head.

If, therefore, the food supply of India were equally distributed, there would be plenty for all. But, owing to the pressure of the increasing population on the soil, and the extreme subdivision of holdings, it is not equally distributed. For example, of the 63 millions of Bengal, including the protected States, 40 millions, as nearly as I can estimate, are well fed; 10 millions suffer hunger when the harvest falls short; and 13 millions are always badly off—in fact, do not know the feeling of a full stomach except in the mango season. An acre of food crops produces, under ordinary circumstances, from 600 to 900 lbs., or much more than is required to feed a man for a year. A Bengal peasant, holding five acres or upwards of land, is reckoned well off, for he can support an average family of four or five persons, and have enough over to pay his rent. But anything under two acres leaves a perilously small margin for a family of four persons. Half an acre yields about 400 lbs. of food in Bengal, and less in other provinces; while the allowance for health and comfort is 450 lbs. per head, besides the rent, clothing, seed, and interest to the village money-lender. Now, there are 24 millions of people in Bengal, who live off 15 millions of acres; and of these, not less than 10 millions, with 3 millions of the worst-off among the landless classes, make up the 13 millions of Bengal, who, notwithstanding the ample food-supply of

634 lbs. per head, scarcely ever lose the sensation of hunger.

The ratio of the permanently hungry population is somewhat smaller in other provinces. Thus, while in Bengal two-thirds of the entire holdings pay less than 10s. of rent, and average about 2½ acres, in Bombay only one-third of the holdings are under 5 acres; while in Madras, one-half the entire holdings pay over 20s. rent at lower rates per acre than those current in Bengal. The pressure of the people on each square mile of Bengal is double the average pressure in Madras and Bombay (including Sind); the holdings are necessarily smaller, and the poverty is more intense. 'A square mile of land in England,' says Mr. Caird, 'highly cultivated, gives employment to 50 persons, in the proportion, 25 men, young and old, and 25 women and boys,' or at the rate of 51 acres to 4 persons. France, with its 180 persons to the square mile, is considered a densely-peopled country, and ten acres of plough land would be reckoned a small holding. Well, there is not a single district in India with only 180 persons to the square mile which is not exceedingly well off; and not a Bengal peasant with ten acres to a family of ten persons who would not be regarded as a fortunate man. An acre of crop-land, under plough cultivation, suffices to keep a human being in comfort; but anything under half an acre means a struggle for life.

The extent of the evil may be thus stated. Two-fifths of the people of British India enjoy a prosperity unknown under native rule; other two-fifths earn a fair but diminishing subsistence; but the remaining fifth, or 40 millions, go through life on insufficient food. It is these underfed 40 millions who form the problem of over-population in India. The difficulty of solving it is intensified by the fact, that in spite of the hard struggle for life, their numbers rapidly increase. 'In ten years,' says Mr. Caird, 'at the present rate of growth, there will be 20 millions more people to feed.'

It may help us to understand the precise dimensions of the problem if we express it in figures. Mr. Caird estimates that the Indian population increases at the rate of 2 millions per annum. If the lot of the people is to be really improved, additional supplies must be provided not only to feed these new mouths, but to furnish a more adequate diet for the already existing ones. This latter task means an annual increase of food sufficient to entirely feed at least half a million, or to double the rations of 1 million of the poorer classes. In this way the lot of 10 millions of these classes would be ameliorated in the course of ten years; and the condition of the whole would be gradually improved in the course of a generation. The initial problem, therefore, is to increase the means of subsistence in India so as to annually feed 2½ millions more people: 2 millions representing the actual increase in numbers, and the ½ million representing a double diet for at least a million of the poorer classes. But figures can only express one aspect of this great social problem. For after providing the additional means of subsistence, it is necessary, if it is to ameliorate the common lot, that it should reach the mouths which most urgently need it. The problem therefore is not only one of supply, but of distribution.

I do not, however, agree with those who think the problem insoluble. The permanent cure for over-population rests with the people themselves, and consists in those restraints upon marriage, to which all nations of small husbandmen have sooner or later to submit. But we cannot wait till that compulsory lesson is learned; for meanwhile, millions will perish. Over-population in India is the direct product of British rule. We have taken on ourselves the responsibility by removing the previous checks upon the increase of the people—checks which, however cruel, are the natural and inevitable ones in Asia, and which take the place of the prudential restraints practised by the peasant-farming races of Europe. We must now discharge that responsibility, and as our own civilised rule has created the difficulty, we must meet it by the resources of civilisation. These resources may lighten the pressure of the population on the soil in three ways,—first, by withdrawing large numbers to non-agricultural industries; second, by distributing the pressure over new or under-populated tracts; third, by increasing the produce of the existing area of cultivation.

In the first direction, something has already been achieved. The new industrial life of India described in the last chapter is already feeding millions of mouths, and before ten years are over it will feed many millions more. India can command the cheapest and most dexterous manufacturing labour in the world.

England can supply the cheapest capital in the world. The household manufactures which were crushed by the co-operation of coal, labour, and capital in England, are now being revived by the co-operation of coal, labour, and capital in India. I believe that we are there at the commencement of a period of manufacturing enterprise which will form an epoch in the history of commerce. We are also apparently on the eve of great mining enterprises. Apart from the gold of Southern India, from the tin, antimony, lead, and mineral oils of Burma; we only await a process for profitably smelting iron with coal having 15 per cent. of ash, in order to create a new industry. No one would have predicted in 1855 that our Indian exports would rise from 20 to close on 70 millions during twenty-five years; and no wise man will now venture to predict the limits of the industrial development of India before the close of this century. But we may with safety assume that the commercial industries of India, for export and home consumption, will distribute, in wages to the labouring classes and in profits to the husbandman, a yearly increase of a million sterling. Now those classes can live well at the rate of £2 a year, for old and young. A million sterling of increased wages and peasant-profits, would therefore represent a comfortable subsistence for an annual increase of half a million of people.

In the second direction, also, something has been done to lighten the pressure of the people on the soil. The emigrants by sea are indeed few, averaging only 18,000 per annum. But there is a tendency for the people to spontaneously spread themselves out to the less thickly-peopled districts. We have only had one census in India, and it will not be possible to gauge the extent of such movements till the next census in 1881. From Column IV. of the table on page 77, it will be seen that a great balance exists of cultivable land not yet brought under the plough. This uncultivable land consists of two classes,—of large blocks or even extensive tracts in sparsely peopled provinces such as Assam, the Punjab, and the central plateau; and of small patches of pasture, jungle, or reclaimable waste interspersed among the closely cultivated districts. The first class opens up a field for migration on a large scale. Hitherto such migrations, although carefully watched by Government, cannot be said to have been fostered by it. A labour-transport department exists, but its object is to secure a high scale of comfort to the coolies *en route*, at the cost of the tea-planters, rather than to encourage both capitalists and labourers in the work of transferring the population from the overcrowded to the underpeopled provinces. The Government is now reconsidering the question in the latter aspect. The transport of labour has, so far, only paid for undertakings yielding a high return, such as tea-planting. That industry now employs 300,000 natives, and feeds about half a million; a large proportion of whom have been brought from densely inhabited tracts to the distant tea-districts.

The problem before Government is how to render labour-transport a paying enterprise for the staple operations of husbandry. It is conceivable that such facilities might be given as would make it profitable for capitalists and land companies to found agricultural settlements in Assam and the Central Provinces. If the landholders of Bengal were thus to turn captains of industry, they would vindicate their position and render it inexpugnable. Thus, among the most thickly peopled parts of India are Bardwán and Darbhangah, each of them held by a Mahárájá. The incomes of these two magnates are popularly reckoned to make a total of over half a million sterling. Well, if the Mahárájá of Bardwán and the Mahárájá of Darbhangah were to obtain suitable facilities from the Government, and to lead forth a colony, each from his own crowded district, by ten days' easy journey to Assam or the Central Provinces, he would not only add to the fortunes of his house, but would set a noble example which other great proprietors in Bengal would not be slow to follow.

Such enterprises already yield a good profit on the hilly outskirts of Bengal and in marshy districts. Half a million of acres have been reclaimed by immigrant colonies in the Sundarbans during the present generation. From personal examination of these clearings, and of the reclaimed tracts in Assam, I am able to say that the task is a lighter one in the latter province. But it requires a capitalist, and above all a native capitalist. A *fakír*, or spiritual person, accompanies each party to pray against the tigers; and receives 1s. 3d. per 100 logs removed in safety. A simple ecclesiastical polity of this sort is found to give confidence and coherence to the immigrants. The Bengal landholder delights to trace his origin to some remote ancestor who came from the north and cut down the jungle. The eponymous village hero is still the man who dug the tank and ploughed up the adjacent fields. Well, the landed gentlemen of Bengal have now a chance of illustrating their families, not by a Brahman-invented pedigree, but by themselves doing what they love to think that their ancestors did—by founding agricultural colonies, and by giving their names to new districts.

The landholders of Bengal are the class which has profited by the increase of population which now forms the great difficulty of Bengal. Many of them have a high sense of their duties; many of them are at present apprehensive that their privileges will be curtailed. Whatever may be the legal basis for those privileges, they have no foundation in the sympathies of their countrymen; and there is a tendency to question that basis among Englishmen both in India and at home. If the great landholders could co-operate with the Government in equalizing the pressure of the population on the soil, they would remove the principal cause which has led to their privileges being challenged. But Government should remember that, in such enterprises, the undertaker risks his capital, and the labourers must be content to risk their health. Hitherto the one object of our labour-transport laws has been to reduce the labourer's risk at the cost of the capitalist. Fifteen years ago, it was my duty to administer those laws in the principal seat of river-embarkation for Assam. The Acts were framed in favour of the coolie, and I administered them, as I was bound to do, in favour of the coolie. At a later period, I had to inquire into the whole operation and spirit of these laws. I came to two conclusions—first, that labour-transport was practicable in Bengal, not only for special industries like tea, but on a great scale for agricultural settlements; second, that if the system were to be re-organized on this new basis, Government must legislate with an eye to the money-risks of the capitalist, as well as to the health-risks of the labourer.

The other class of unoccupied land consists not of large blocks, but of patches interspersed among closely cultivated districts. A glance at the table on page 77 will show how vast an aggregate must exist of this class. 'There is,' write the Famine Commissioners, 'in most villages, scope for a slow and gradual extension of cultivation by the breaking-up of uncultivated land; and outside the village areas there is an immense extent which is more or less fit for cultivation.' How rapidly the process goes on, may be realized from the fact that the Madras peasantry increased their cultivated fields from 12 to 20 millions of acres, in the quarter of a century ending 1878. In truth, the process goes on too rapidly. For the cultivable waste comprises the pasture lands on which the village herds graze, and the patches of jungle on which the people depend for fuel. Now, as we have seen, the lack of pasture and the substitution of cow-manure for firewood, are main factors in the exhaustion of the Indian soil.

While, therefore, much may be done by migration

to unoccupied tracts, and by the tillage of waste patches of land, the latter process drives us back upon the third means of augmenting the food-supply, mentioned at p. 81, namely by increasing the produce of the existing area of cultivation. And here we are met at the outset by a statement often repeated, and which the *Hindu Patriot* lately put in very pithy words: 'The native cultivators have nothing to learn so far as non-scientific agriculture is concerned, and the adoption of scientific agriculture is wholly beyond their means.' I had the good fortune, in my youth, to work during two years in the laboratory of the greatest agricultural chemist of that day. If the only alternative lay between a strictly scientific and an altogether unscientific husbandry, I should have to concur in the *Hindu Patriot's* conclusion. But the choice is not thus limited. I have compared the high farming of the Lothians with the primitive tillage of the Argyleshire glens, and I find that both these extremes are essentially local. The husbandry of England and of Europe occupies a shifting position between the two. One little improvement takes place in one district, another small change for the better in another. Every one knows that strictly scientific farming trebles the produce; that a field which produces 730 lbs. of wheat without manure can be made to yield 2342 lbs. by manure. But every one also knows that the native of India has neither the capital nor the knowledge required to attain this result. If, therefore, the problem before him was to increase his crops threefold, I should despair of his success. But, as I shall now show, the problem is not to increase the food-supply of India by 300 per cent. at a stroke, but by 1½ per cent. a year.

Wheat-land in the North-Western Provinces, which now gives only 840 lbs. an acre, yielded 1140 lbs. in the time of Akbar, and would be made to produce 1800 lbs. in East Norfolk. The average return of food-grains in India shows about 700 lbs. per acre; in England, wheat averages over 1700 lbs. The Secretary to the Government of India, in its late Department of Agriculture, declares, 'that with proper manuring and proper tillage, every acre, broadly speaking, of land in the country can be made to yield 30, 50, or 70 per cent. more of every kind of crop than it at present produces; and with a fully corresponding increase in the profits of cultivation.' But, as I shall now show, a yearly increase of 1½ per cent. would suffice.

The food-supply of India must be augmented so as to allow of an annual increase of 2½ millions of people. This rate, as explained at p. 80, will not only feed the new mouths, but will ameliorate the condition of the existing population. Now 2½ millions are less than 1½ per cent. of the present population, and the present food-supply is more than that population consumes. If, therefore, we add 1½ per cent. yearly to the food-production, the supply will more than keep pace with the increased demand upon it, so far as the internal wants of India are concerned. I shall specify four out of many considerations which make me believe that, without attempting any flights in scientific farming, it is possible to steadily increase the Indian food-supply to the extent of 1½ per cent. per annum.

The first impediment to better husbandry is the fewness and weakness of the cattle. 'Over a great portion of the Empire,' writes the Secretary to the late Agricultural Department in India, 'the mass of the cattle are starved for six weeks every year. The hot winds roar, every green thing has disappeared, no hot-weather forage is grown; the last year's fodder has generally been consumed in keeping the well-bullocks on their legs during the irrigation of the spring crops; and all the husbandman can do is just to keep his poor brutes alive on the chopped leaves of the few trees and shrubs he has access to, the roots of grass and herbs that he digs out of the edges of fields, and the like. In good years he just succeeds; in bad years the weakly ones die of starvation. But then come the rains. Within the week, as though by magic, the burning sands are carpeted with rank, luscious herbage, the cattle *will* eat and over-eat, and millions die of one form or other of cattle disease, springing out of this starvation followed by sudden repletion with rank, juicy, immature herbage.' He estimates 'the average annual loss of cattle in India by preventable disease' at 10 million beasts, worth 7½ millions sterling. He complains that no real attempt has been made either to bring veterinary knowledge within reach of the people, or to organize a system of village plantation which would feed their cattle through the summer.

The second impediment to improved husbandry is

the want of manure. If there were more stock, there would be more manure, and the absence of firewood compels the people to use even the scanty droppings of their existing cattle for fuel. Under such circumstances agriculture ceases to be the manufacture of food, and becomes a mere spoliation of the soil. Forage crops, such as lucerne, guinea-grass, and the great stemmed millets, might furnish an immense weight to the acre. Government is now considering whether their cultivation could not be promoted by reducing the irrigation rates on green fodder crops. A system of village plantations would not only supply firewood, but would yield leaves and an undergrowth of fodder sufficient to tide the cattle over their six weeks' struggle for life each summer. In some districts Government has land of its own which it could thus plant; in others it is only a sleeping partner in the soil. The system would have to be considerately organized on a legislative basis, but Mr. Hume, the highest authority on such a subject, declares the system perfectly practicable. For the details I refer the reader to his valuable pamphlet on 'Agricultural Reform in India.' In Switzerland, I found that the occupiers of *allmends*, or communal lands, have at least in some cantons to keep up a certain number of trees. It seems a fair question whether plantations ought not in many parts of India to be now made an incident of the land-tenure; they would go far to solve the two fundamental difficulties of Indian agriculture—the loss of cattle, and the want of manure.

Meanwhile, the natives set an increasing value on

manure. The great cities are being converted from centres of disease into sources of food-supply. For a time, caste prejudices stood in the way of utilizing the night-soil. 'Five years ago,' writes the Secretary to the Poona Municipality, 'agriculturists would not touch the *poudrette* when prepared, and could not be induced to take it away at even a nominal charge. At present the out-turn of manure is not enough to keep pace with the demand, and the peasants buy it up from four to six months in advance.' At Amritsar, in the Punjab, 30,000 donkey-loads were sold in one year. A great margin still exists for economy, both in the towns and villages; but the husbandman is becoming more alive to the utilization of every source of manure, and his prejudices are gradually giving way under the stern pressure of facts.

The third impediment to improved agriculture in India is the want of water. Mr. Caird, the chief English authority who has inquired into the subject, believes that if only one-third of the cultivated area were irrigated, India would be secure against famine. At any rate, an extension of irrigation would alone suffice to raise the food-supply by more than 1½ per cent. during many years. Since India passed to the Crown, great progress has been made in this direction. Money has been invested by millions of pounds; 200,000 millions of acres are now under irrigation; and in the five British provinces which require it most, 28 per cent. of the area, or say one-third, is artificially supplied with water. Those Provinces are the Punjab, the North-

West, Oudh, Sind, and Madras. Looking to what has of late years been done, and to what yet remains to be done by wells and petty works with the aid of loans from the State, I think we may reckon on a vast increase of food from irrigation.

I shall mention only one more means of improving Indian tillage. The Indian Government is the greatest landed proprietor in the world; it is, I think, the only Government of a people of husbandmen which has no Agricultural Department. From the first, it concentrated its attention on its own share of the crops, and interested itself too little in their cultivation. Ten years ago, Lord Mayo, the only Indian Viceroy who had ever farmed for a livelihood, founded an Agricultural Department in India. But the traditions of Indian administration were too strong for him. His Agricultural Department soon became a Revenue Department, and before long was abolished. I do not think that any official *deus ex machinâ* can bring down an *avatâr* of steam ploughs and chemical manures upon India. But I watched the operations of the late Agricultural Department, and I have studied the practical work done at its model farms. I believe it capable, by continuous effort, of slowly but surely effecting great improvements in Indian husbandry. Food production depends on three elements—labour, land, and capital. We have abundance of labour in India: there is still enough land if the population could be equally distributed over it; and the Government has unlimited cheap capital at its command, if it had only the knowledge and supervision requisite for its safe application to the soil. India has entered on the inevitable change which takes place in all countries from 'extensive' to 'intensive' husbandry, as the population increases. It has been my duty to find out precisely what amount of information exists with regard to the agriculture of India; and to compare that information with the facts which the Governments of Europe and America supply on the same points. I have come to the conclusion that no central Government stands more in need of agricultural knowledge than the Government of India, and that no Government has a smaller stock of such knowledge within its central body. I rejoice, therefore, that the Famine Commissioners urge the re-establishment of an Agricultural Department in India.

I have now set forth the problem of an increased food-supply for India; endeavoured to state its exact dimensions; and shown that, while it demands organized efforts on a great scale, it is quite capable of solution. The problem, however, is not only one of supply, but of distribution. By one set of efforts the food must be increased; another set of efforts must secure a fair share of that food to the actual tiller of the soil. In Southern India, as I have mentioned, the cry of the peasantry is for protection against the money-lenders. After a careful inquiry, the Government determined to respond to that cry. It has practically said to the village bankers: 'A state of things has grown up under British rule which enables you to push the cultivators, by means of our Courts, to extremities unknown under the native dynasties, and repugnant to the customs of India. Henceforth, in considering the security on which you lend money, please to know that the peasant cannot be imprisoned or sold out of his farm to satisfy your claims; and we shall free him from the life-long burden of those claims by a mild bankruptcy law.' Such is the gist of the Southern India Agriculturists' Relief Act of 1879.

It provides, in the first place, for small rural debtors of £5 and under. If the Court is satisfied that such a debtor is really unable to pay the whole sum, it may direct the payment of such portion as it considers that he can pay, and grant him a discharge for the balance. To debtors for larger amounts, it gives the protection of an Insolvency Act. No agriculturist shall henceforth be arrested or imprisoned in execution of a decree for money. In addition to the old provisions against the sale of the necessary implements of his trade, no agriculturist's immoveable property shall be attached or sold in execution of any decree, unless it has been specifically mortgaged for the debt to which such decree relates. But even when it has been specifically mortgaged, the Court may order the debtor's holding to be cultivated, for a period not exceeding seven years, on behalf of the creditor, after allowing a sufficient portion of it for the support of the debtor and his family. At the end of the seven years the debtor is discharged. If the debtor himself applies for relief under the Insolvency clauses, the procedure is as follows:—His moveable property, less the implements of his trade, are liable to sale for his debts. His immoveable property, or farm, is divided into two parts, one of which is set aside as 'required for the support of the insolvent and members of his family dependent on him,' while the remainder is to be managed on behalf of his creditors. But 'nothing in this section shall authorize the Court to take into possession any houses or other buildings belonging to, and occupied by, an agriculturist.' Village arbitrators or 'conciliators' are appointed by the same Act, and every creditor must first try to settle his claims before them. If the effort at arbitration fails, the 'conciliator' shall give the applicant a certificate to that effect. No suit to which an agriculturist (residing within any local area to which a 'conciliator' has been appointed) is a party, shall be entertained by any Civil Court, unless the plaintiff produces a certificate from the 'conciliator' that arbitration has been attempted and failed.

Much may be said on general principles against this Act, and much also may be said for it under the special conditions in which the South Indian peasant now finds himself placed. On the one hand, it gives a protection to the ignorant cultivator such as he practically enjoyed under Native rule, when the money-lender could not sell his holding, because there was more land than there were husbandmen to till it. But on the other hand, it increases the risks in the application of capital to land. It secures the idle or extravagant cultivator from the consequence of his own acts, and thus tends to arrest that process of riddling out the thriftless members of the population, which, however cruel in its action, results in bringing the soil into the hands able to make the most of it.

While in Southern India the demand is thus for restraints upon the money-lender, in Bengal the cry of the peasantry is for protection against the landlord. Accordingly, in 1859, the Government practically said to the landholders: 'We created you as a proprietary body in 1793 by our own act. In doing so, we made over to you valuable rights which up to that time were vested in the State, but we carefully reserved the rights of the cultivators. We shall now ascertain and define the rights of the cultivators; and we shall settle your relations with them on the basis of those rights.' The result was embodied in the famous Land Law of 1859, which divided the cultivators of Bengal into four classes:—First, those who had held their holdings at the same rates since 1793, and whose rents could not be raised at all. Second, those who had held their land at the same rent for twenty years, and were therefore presumed by law to have held since 1793, unless the contrary was proved. Third, those who had held for twelve years. Such tenants had a right of occupancy, and their rents could be raised only for certain specified reasons by a suit at law. Fourth, those who had held for less than twelve years, and were left to make what bargain they could with the landlords.

Further experience, since 1859, has taught the Government that even these provisions are inadequate to avert the wholesale enhancement of rents in Bengal. It accordingly issued a Commission in 1879 to inquire into the questions involved; and the report of the Commission has just reached England. Whatever may be the fate of the draft law which these folios propose, they will remain a monument of noble intention, able discussion of principles, and honest statement of the facts. The Commissioners of 1879, like the legislators of 1859, have arrived at the conclusion that a substantial peasant-right in the soil exists in Bengal. They would confirm all the rights given to the peasant by the Land Code of 1859, and they propose to augment them. The first class of cultivators, who have held their land at the same rates since 1793, can never have their rent raised. The second class, or those who have thus held for twenty years, are still presumed to have held since 1793. The third class of cultivators, who have held for twelve years, have their privileges increased. Their occupancy rights are to be consolidated into a valuable peasant-tenure, transferable by sale, gift, or inheritance; and it is proposed that all increase in the value of the land or the crop, not arising from the agency of either the landlord or tenant, shall henceforth be divided equally between them. This provision is a very important one in a country like Bengal, where new railways, new roads, and the increase of the people and of trade, constantly tend to raise the price of the agricultural staples. What political economists call the 'unearned increment,' is no longer to accrue to the proprietor, but is to be divided between him and the cultivator; so that landlord and tenant are henceforth to be joint sharers in the increasing value of the land.

But the great changes proposed by the Rent Commissioners of 1879 refer to the fourth or lowest class of husbandmen, who have held for less than twelve years, and whom the Land Code of 1859 admitted to no rights whatever. The Commissioners declare that the competition for land, if unchecked by law or custom, will reduce 'the whole agricultural population to a condition of misery and degradation;' and they have resolved, so far as in them lies, to arrest this slow ruin of Bengal. They enunciate the principle that 'the land of a country belongs to the people of a country; and while vested rights should be treated with all possible tenderness, no mode of appropriation and cultivation should be permanently allowed by the ruler, which involves the wretchedness of the great majority of the community; if the alteration or amendment of the law relating to land can by itself, or in conjunction with other measures, obviate or remedy the misfortune.'

Strong doctrine this; and very stringently do the Commissioners apply it. In their draft code, they propose a system of compensation for disturbance whose thorough-going character contrasts strongly with the mild Irish Bill which the House of Lords rejected last session. The Bengal Rent Commissioners would accord a quasi-occupancy right to all tenants who have held for three years. If the landlord demands an increased rent from such a tenant, and the tenant prefers to leave rather than submit to the enhancement, then the landlord must pay him, first, a substantial compensation for disturbance, and second, a substantial compensation for improvements. The compensation for disturbance is calculated at a sum equal to one year's increased rent, as demanded by the landlord. The compensation for improvements includes payment for buildings erected by the tenant, for tanks, wells, irrigation works, drainage works, embankments, or for the renewal or improvement of any of the foregoing; also for any land which the tenant may have reclaimed or enclosed, and for all fruit trees which he may have planted. The operation of these clauses will be, that before the landlord can raise the rent, he must be prepared to pay to the out-going tenant a sum which will swallow up the increased rental for several years.

The practical result is to give tenant-right to all cultivators who have held their land for three years or upwards — that is, to the mass of the people in Bengal. Whether these stringent provisions become law remains to be seen. For we must remember that the landlords have rights as well as the tenants. But before the Commissioners' suggestions can become law, they must obtain the assent, successively, of the Provincial Government of Bengal, of the Governor-General in Council, of the Indian Legislature, and finally of the Secretary of State who represents the majority in the British Parliament. At each of these stages, the vested rights of the landholders will be carefully considered, and the arguments on which the proposed changes are based will be threshed out.

While the efforts of the Indian executive are directed to the increase of the food-supply, the Legislature is thus endeavouring to secure a fair share of that supply to the tiller of the soil.

The analogy of the situation in Bengal to the agrarian agitation in Ireland, is in some respects a striking one. In both countries, a state of things has grown up under British rule which seems unbearable to a section of the people. In Bengal, the peasantry have fought by every weapon of delay afforded by the courts; in England, the Irish representatives are fighting by every form of obstruction possible in Parliament. In both countries we may disapprove of the weapons employed; but in both we must admit that these weapons are better than the ruder ones of physical force. In neither can the Government parley with outrage or crime. In both countries, I believe that the peasantry will more or less completely win the day; for in both, the state of things of which they complain is repugnant to the awakened conscience of the British nation. But the analogy, although striking, must not be pushed too far. For on the one hand, the Irish peasantry has emigration open to it—a resource practically not available to the Bengal husbandman. On the other hand, the proprietary right in Bengal was a gift of our own as late as 1793—a gift hedged in by reservations in favour of the peasantry, and conferred for the distinctly expressed purpose of securing the welfare of the people. The proprietary right in Ireland is the growth of centuries of spoliation and conquest. It may, perhaps, be found possible to accord a secure position to the peasantry of Bengal without injustice to the landlords. The Irish difficulty, although on a smaller scale, is complicated by old wrongs.

One comfort we may derive from our experience in Bengal. It is, that the land laws, if rightly dealt with, form an ordinary and a necessary subject for legislative improvement in countries like India and Ireland, where the mass of the people live by the tillage of the soil. The reform of the existing tenures is, therefore, a matter for legislation, not for revolution. The problem, alike in India and in Ireland, is how to do the best for the peasant at the least cost to the State, and with the least infringement of vested proprietary rights.

IV. THE MAINTENANCE OF A GOVERNMENT ON EUROPEAN STANDARDS OF EFFICIENCY FROM AN ASIATIC SCALE OF REVENUE.

I HAVE endeavoured to explain the real meaning of the poverty of the Indian people. I shall now ask attention to some of the difficulties which that poverty gives rise to in the government of the country. Men must first have enough to live upon before they can pay taxes. The revenue-yielding powers of a nation are regulated, not by its numbers, but by the margin between its national earnings and its requirements for subsistence. It is because this margin is so great in England that the English are the most taxable people in the world. It is because this margin is so small in India that any increase in the revenue involves serious difficulties. The 34 millions of our countrymen in Great Britain and Ireland pay their 68 millions sterling of Imperial taxation* with far greater ease than the 190 millions of British

* Customs, 20 millions; Inland revenue, 48 millions: total taxation, 68 millions. The *gross* revenue of the United Kingdom in 1880 is £81,265,055, besides £29,247,595 of local taxation; total, £110,512,650.

subjects in India pay an actual taxation of 35 millions. It may seem a contradiction in terms to say that the English, who pay at the rate of forty shillings per head to the Imperial exchequer, besides many local burdens, are more lightly taxed than the Indians, who pay only at the rate of 3s. 8d. per head to the Imperial exchequer, with scarcely any local burdens. But the sum of forty shillings per head bears a much smaller proportion to the margin between the national earnings and the national requirements for subsistence in England, than the sum of 3s. 8d. bears to that margin in India. In estimating the revenue-yielding powers of India, we must get rid of the delusive influence which hundreds of millions of tax-payers exercise upon the imagination. We must think less of the numbers and more of the poverty of the Indian people.

But while anxious that the gravity of our financial situation in India should be realized, I do not think that any good can come of exaggerating it. At this moment we are taking less taxation from the Indian people than was taken by their own Asiatic rulers. The following table (p. 104) shows the revenues of the Mughal Empire from the reign of Akbar in 1593 to its practical downfall in 1761. The figures are derived from many independent sources,—from returns drawn up by skilful English officers of the East India Company; from the materials afforded by the Native Revenue Survey, and the Mughal exchequer accounts; from the reports of European travellers; and from the financial statement of the Empire as presented to the Afghán conqueror, Ahmad

Revenues of the Mughal Emperors at Thirteen Various Periods from 1593 to 1761,* from a Smaller Area and Population than those of British India.

	Mughal Emperors.	Authority.	Land Revenue.	Revenue from all Sources.
1	Akbar, A.D. 1593, . .	Nizám-ud-dín Ahmad: not for all India,	...	£32,000,000
		Allowance for Provincial Troops (*búmí*),†	...	10,000,000 †
				nett £42,000,000
2	,, 1594, . .	Abul Fazl MSS.: not for all India, . .	*nett* £16,574,388	...
3	,, ,, . .	Official Documents: not for all India, .	*nett* 16,582,440	...
4	,, 1605, . .	Indian Authorities quoted by De Läet, .	*nett* 17,450,000	...
5	Jahángír, 1609–11, .	Captain Hawkins, ...	...	*nett* 50,000,000
6	,, 1628, . .	Abdul Hamíd Láhorí, ...	*nett* 17,500,000	...
7	Sháh Jahán, 1648–9, .	,, ...	*nett* 22,000,000	...
8	Aurangzeb, 1655, . .	Official Documents, ...	*gross* 26,743,970	...
			nett 24,056,114	...
9	,, 1670? . .	Later Official Documents, . . .	*gross* 35,641,431	...
			nett 34,505,890	...
10	,, 1695, . .	Gemelli Careri, ...	...	*nett* 80,000,000
11	,, 1697, . .	Manucci (Catrou), ...	*nett* 38,719,400	*nett* 77,438,800
12	,, 1707, . .	Ramusis, ...	*nett* 30,179,692	...
13	Sháh Alam, 1761, .	Official Statement presented to Ahmad Sháh Abdáli on his entering Delhi, .	*nett* 34,506,640	...

* The above Table is reproduced from Mr. Edward Thomas' *Revenue Resources of the Mughal Empire*, published in 1871, and has been revised by him from materials which he has collected since that date.

† This is the lowest estimate at which the *Búmí* or Landwehr, in contradistinction to the Royal Army, can be reckoned.—Mr. Thomas' *Revenue Resources of the Mughal Empire*, p. 12. I insert the words *nett* and *gross* by his direction.

Sháh Abdáli, on his entry into Delhi. One of the most learned numismatists of our day, Mr. Edward Thomas, has devoted a treatise to sifting these materials, and I reproduce his results. Indeed, the difficulty of a comparison has arisen, not from the absence of information in respect to the Mughal revenues, but from want of exact statements regarding our own. As I pointed out at Birmingham in 1879, the Parliamentary Indian Accounts are rendered in such a form as to permit of the widest assertions regarding Indian taxation, varying from an annual total of 34 to over 60 millions sterling. Efforts have since then been made to remedy this, and a statement lately presented to Parliament exhibits the actual revenue and expenditure of British India during a series of years.

From this authoritative statement I find that the taxation of British India, during the ten years ending 1879, has averaged 35⅓ millions per annum. That is the gross sum, as shown in the table on next page; the net would be less: say for purposes of easy recollection, 35 millions sterling, or 3s. 8d. per head. From the table on last page we see that in 1593, when the Mughal Empire was of much less extent and much less populous than our own, the burdens of the people amounted, under Akbar, to 42 millions sterling. Captain Hawkins, from careful inquiries at Agra, returned the revenue of Akbar's successor in 1609 at 50 millions. At the end of that century, we have two separate returns for 1695 and 1697, giving the revenues of Aurangzeb respectively at 80 and 77½ millions.

GROSS TAXATION OF BRITISH INDIA.

	1869-70.	1870-71.	1871-72.	1872-73.	1873-74.	1874-75.	1875-76.	1876-77.	1877-78.	1878-79.
	£	£	£	£	£	£	£	£	£	£
Land Revenue, . .	21,088,019	20,622,823	20,520,337	21,348,669	21,037,912	21,296,793	21,503,742	19,857,152	19,869,667	22,330,586
Excise, ...	2,253,655	2,374,465	2,369,109	2,323,788	2,286,637	2,346,143	2,493,232	2,523,045	2,457,075	2,619,349
Assessed Taxes, . .	1,110,224	2,072,025	825,241	580,139	20,136	2,747	510	310	86,110	900,920
Provincial Rates, . .	...	...	...	...	...	...	...	...	238,504	2,638,835
Customs, . . .	2,429,185	2,610,789	2,575,990	2,653,890	2,628,495	2,678,479	2,721,389	2,483,345	2,622,296	2,326,561
Salt, ...	5,888,707	6,106,280	5,966,595	6,165,630	6,150,662	6,227,301	6,244,415	6,304,658	6,460,082	6,941,120
Stamps, . . .	2,379,316	2,510,316	2,476,333	2,608,512	2,699,936	2,758,042	2,835,368	2,838,628	2,993,483	3,110,540
Total, .	£35,149,106	36,296,698	34,733,605	35,680,628	34,823,778	35,309,505	35,798,656	34,007,138	34,727,217	40,867,911

Total for Ten Years ending 1879, ...	£357,394,242
Deduct Refunds, Drawbacks, and adjusting Payments, as per Parliamentary Statement, ...	4,379,234
Taxation for Ten Years ending 1879, . . .	£353,015,008
Yearly Average, ...	£35,301,100

If we examine the items in the Mughal accounts, we find the explanation of their enormous totals. The land tax then, as now, formed about one-half of the whole revenue. The net land revenue demand of the Mughal Empire averaged 25 millions sterling from 1593 to 1761; or 32 millions during the last century of that Empire, from 1655 to 1761. The annual *net* land revenue raised from the much larger area of British India during the ten years ending 1879, has been 18 millions sterling (*gross*, 21 millions). But besides the land revenue there were under our predecessors not less than forty imposts of a personal character. They included taxes upon religious assemblies, upon trees, upon marriage, upon the peasant's hearth, and upon his cattle. How severe some of them were, may be judged from the Poll Tax. For the purposes of this tax, the non-Muhammadan population was divided into three classes, paying respectively £4, £2, and £1 annually to the Exchequer for each adult male. The lowest of these rates, if now levied from each non-Musalmán male adult, would alone yield an amount exceeding our whole Indian taxation. Yet, under the Mughal Empire, the Poll Tax was only one of forty burdens.

We may briefly sum up the results as follows. Under the Mughal Empire from 1593 to 1761, the Imperial demand averaged about 60 millions sterling a year. During the past ten years ending 1879, the Imperial taxation of British India, with its far larger population, averaged 35 millions. Under the Mughal Empire, the land tax between 1655 and 1761 averaged 32 millions.

Under the British Empire, the net land tax has, during the past ten years, averaged 18 millions.

Not only is the taxation of British India much less than that raised by the Mughal emperors, but it compares favourably with the taxation of other Asiatic countries in our own days. The only other Empire in Asia which pretends to a civilised government is Japan. I have no special acquaintance with the Japanese revenues; but I find from German writers that over 11 millions sterling are there raised from a population of 34 million people, or deducting certain items, a taxation of about 6s. a head. In India, where we try to govern on a higher standard of efficiency, the rate of actual taxation is 3s. 8d. a head.

If, instead of dealing with the Imperial revenues as a whole, we concentrate our survey on any one Province, we find these facts brought out in a still stronger light. To take a single instance. After a patient scrutiny of the records, I found that, allowing for the change in the value of money, the ancient revenue of Orissa represented eight times the quantity of the staple food which our own revenue now represents.* The native revenue of Orissa supported a magnificent court with a crowded seraglio, swarms of priests, a large army, and a costly public worship. Under our rule, Orissa does little more than defray the local cost of protecting person and property, and of its irrigation works. In Orissa, the Rájá's share of the crops amounted, with dues,

* The evidence on which these statements are based, was published in my *Orissa*, vol. i. pp. 323-329: Smith, Elder, & Co. 1872.

to 60 per cent., and the mildest Native Governments demanded 33 per cent. The Famine Commissioners estimate the land tax in the British Provinces 'at from 3 per cent. to 7 per cent. of the gross out-turn.' Ample deductions are allowed for the cost of cultivation, the risks of the season, the maintenance of the husbandman and his family. Of the balance which remains, Government nominally takes one-half; but how small a proportion this bears to the crop may be seen from the returns collected by the Famine Commissioners. Their figures deal with 176 out of the 191 millions of our Indian fellow-subjects. These 176 millions cultivate 188 millions of acres, grow 331 millions sterling worth of produce, and now pay 18¾ millions of land revenue. While, therefore, they raise over £1, 15s. 0d. worth of produce per acre, they pay to Government under 2s. of land tax per acre. Instead of thus paying 5½ per cent. as they do to us, they would under the Mughal rule have been called upon to pay from 33 to 50 per cent. of the crop. The two systems, indeed, proceed upon entirely different principles. The Native Governments, write the Famine Commissioners, often taxed the land 'to the extent of taking from the occupier the whole of the surplus' 'after defraying the expenses of cultivation.' The British Government objects to thus 'sweeping off the whole margin of profit.'

What becomes of the surplus which our Government declines to take? It goes to feed an enormously increased population. The tax-gatherer now leaves so large a margin to the husbandman, that the province of Bengal, for example, feeds three times as many mouths as it did in 1780, and has a vast surplus of produce, over and above its own wants, for exportation. 'In the majority of Native Governments,' writes the greatest living authority on the question,* 'the revenue officer takes all he can get; and would take treble the revenue we should assess, if he were strong enough to exact it. In ill-managed States, the cultivators are relentlessly squeezed: the difference between the Native system and ours being, mainly, that the cultivator in a Native State is seldom or never sold up, and that he is usually treated much as a good bullock is treated; *i.e.*, he is left with enough to feed and clothe him and his family, so that they may continue to work.' John Stuart Mill studied the condition of the Indian people more deeply than any other political economist, and he took an indulgent view of Native institutions. His verdict upon the Mughal Government is that, 'except during the occasional accident of a humane and vigorous local administrator, the exactions had no practical limit but the inability of the peasant to pay more.'

Throughout British India, the landed classes pay revenue at the rate of 5s. 6d. per head, including the land tax for their farms, or 1s. 9d. without it. The trading classes pay 3s. 3d. per head; the artisans, 2s.—equal to four days' wages in the year; and the agricul-

* Mr. Alfred Lyall, C.B., formerly Governor-General's Agent in Rájputána, and now Foreign Secretary to the Government of India; quoted in the Despatch of the Governor-General in Council to the Secretary of State, 8th June 1880. 'Condition of India,' Blue Book, pp. 36-37.

tural labourers, 1s. 8d. The whole taxation, including the Government rent for the land, averaged, as we have seen, 3s. 8d. per head, during the ten years ending 1879. But the Famine Commissioners declare that 'any native of India who does not trade or own land, and who chooses to drink no spirituous liquor, and to use no English cloth or iron, need pay in taxation only about sevenpence a year on account of the salt he consumes. On a family of three persons, the charge amounts to 1s. 9d., or about four days' wages of a labouring man and his wife.'

The weak point of our financial position in India is not that we take more from the people than their Native rulers did, but that what we take barely suffices for the cost of our administration. Each petty provincial prince under the Mughal Empire spent as much on his personal pomp and luxury, as now suffices for all the expense of the British Viceroy of India and his Council. But our Government, although less magnificent, rests upon a more costly basis. For the treasures, which under the Mughal dynasties were concentrated upon the palaces and harems of the rulers, are by us scattered broadcast in securing protection to the ruled. No previous Government of India ever kept up an army on such a scale of efficiency as to render invasion and piratical devastation impossible from without, and to absolutely put down internecine wars and the predatory nations within. Those invasions and depredations ruined thousands of homesteads every year. But the idea of such an army, paid like ours from the Imperial exchequer, would have been dismissed as an impossible dream by the most powerful of the Mughal emperors. Well, we keep up such an army, and it does its work at an average cost of 1s. 8d. a head of the Indian population. This may seem a moderate sum. It is not one-twentieth part of the 40s. per head paid by the population of the United Kingdom; but it represents nearly one-half of the whole actual taxation which we take from the Indian people. No Native dynasty ever attempted to develop the resources of India by a network of communications. Some of the emperors constructed great military highways, but the idea of systematically opening out every district of India by commercial trade-routes, by roads, railways, and navigable canals, is a purely British idea. The outlay will reimburse the Indian tax-payer a hundredfold, but meanwhile the railways alone have saddled him with a debt of 120 millions sterling; while many public works are profitable rather by their indirect consequences on trade or agriculture, than by any direct yield to the revenues.

No Mughal emperor ever mapped out India for judicial purposes, assigning to each small district a court of justice maintained from the Imperial exchequer. The district records show that when we obtained the country, the people had simply to settle their disputes among themselves; which the landholders did very profitably by bands of *lathiáls* or club-men, and the peasantry with the aid of trial by ordeal, the divining rod, and boiling oil. Where a law officer existed in the rural districts, he was not a salaried judge drawing his monthly pay from the Treasury, and watched by superior courts, but a mere seller of decisions dependent for his livelihood on the payments of the litigants. The police of the Mughal Empire were an undisciplined, half-starved soldiery, who lived upon the people. The officer in charge of the local troops was also the chief magistrate of his district; and the criminal courts of the East India Company long retained their old Mughal appellation of the Faujdárí, or 'army department.' The idea of prison as a place of reformatory discipline never entered the minds of these soldier-magistrates. Our early officers found the Muhammadan jails crowded with wretched men whose sole sentence was 'to remain during pleasure,'—a legal formula which, translated into honest English, meant until the harpies of the court had squeezed the prisoner's friends of their uttermost farthing. The prisons themselves were ruinous hovels, whose inmates had to be kept in stocks and fetters, or were held down flat under bamboos, not on account of their crimes, but, to use the words of an official report of 1792, 'because from the insecurity of the jails, the jailor had no other means of preventing their escape.' No Mughal emperor ever conceived the idea of giving public instruction as a State duty to all his subjects. He might raise a marble mosque in honour of God and himself, lavish millions on a favourite lady's tomb, or grant lands to learned men of his own religion; but the task of educating the whole Indian people, rich and poor, of whatever race, or caste, or creed, was never attempted.

In these, as in other departments, the English have had to build up, from the very foundations, the fabric of a civilised government. The material framework for such a government, its court-houses, public buildings, barracks, jails, hospitals, and schools, have cost not less than a hundred millions sterling. But the revolution in the inward spirit of the administration has involved a far greater and more permanent expenditure than this reconstruction of its outward and material fabric. We have had to re-organize a government, conceived in the interests of the pomp and luxury of the few, into a government conceived in the interests of the well-being and security of the many. The vast outlay thus involved may be realized from three items —justice, police, and education. As regards the dispensing of justice, rural tribunals, maintained by the State, scarcely existed when we obtained the country in the last century. One of the earliest acts of the East India Company was to create such tribunals. Well, I have taken six districts at hazard from my Statistical Account of Bengal, and I find that the Company allowed about the end of the last century 19 courts of justice for these six districts. The Queen's Government of India in 1870 maintained 161 courts of justice in those six districts. The demand for accessible justice constantly becomes more exacting. Thus, in eight districts, for which in 1850 the Company allowed 176 courts of justice, 288 courts had to be provided in

1870, and further additions have since been made. Justice has been brought very near to the door of the peasant. But it has cost the Government many millions sterling to do so; and the gross outlay has risen from under 1¾ millions in 1857, during the last year of the Company, to over 3⅓ millions during the present year 1880, or twofold.

The police of India has, in like manner, been completely re-organized since the Government passed under the Crown. The general force was reconstructed on a new basis by Act V. of 1861. The Muhammadans bequeathed to us in the previous century a police which I have described from the manuscript records as 'an enormous ragged army who ate up the industry of the province.'* The Company had improved this police so far as to spend a million sterling upon it in its last year, 1857. The re-organized police of India now costs, in 1880, a gross sum exceeding 2½ millions sterling, or more than twofold. As regards education, no system of public instruction existed either under the Mughal emperors or under the East India Company. Sir Charles Wood's justly famous despatch, which laid the foundation of the enlightenment of India, was only penned in 1854. The Company had not time to give effect to that despatch before its rule disappeared; and the vast system of public instruction which is now educating two millions of our eastern fellow-subjects, is the work of the Queen's Government in India. It is a noble work, but it has cost money. In going over

* *Annals of Rural Bengal*, 5th ed. p. 335.

the items of Indian expenditure, the single one which I find steadily increases from year to year is the expenditure on education. It now exceeds a gross sum of a million sterling per annum from the Imperial revenues, with perhaps double that sum from fees and local sources. I cite only three examples of the increased cost of a Government conducted according to European standards of efficiency, but from those three items you may not unfairly judge of the increased cost of every other department.

Take Justice, Police, and Education, and you will find that the East India Company in 1857 gave less than 3 millions worth of these commodities to its subjects in the last year of its rule, while the Queen's Government now spends a gross sum of nearly 7 millions sterling upon them. No one will grudge a rupee of the extra 4 millions sterling thus spent in educating the people of India, in protecting their persons and property, and in hearing their complaints. Nor, I think, can any of us grudge another large item of expenditure, almost unknown in the time of the Company, but which is now estimated at an annual charge of 1½ millions sterling, namely, the relief of the peasantry during famine. The truth is, that we have suddenly applied our own English ideas of what a good government should do, to an Asiatic country where the people pay not one-tenth per head of the English rate of taxation. It is easy to govern efficiently at a cost of forty shillings per head as in England; but the problem in India is how to attain the same standard of efficiency at a cost of

3s. 8d. a head. That is the sum in proportion which one finance minister after another is called to work out. Every year the Indian finance minister has to provide for more schools, more police, more courts, more hospitals, more roads, more railways, more canals. In short, every year he has to spend more money in bringing up the Indian administration to the English standard of efficiency. The money is well spent, but it has to be found, and there are only two ways by which a finance minister can find it.

He must either cut down existing expenditure, or he must increase the taxation. As a matter of fact, the finance ministers of India have done both. During the twenty-two years since India passed to the Crown, they have abolished one highly-paid place after another. Under the Company, the civil and military services of India were regarded as roads to an assured fortune. Those services now yield very little more than suffices for a man to discharge the duties of the position in which he may be placed. While the higher salaries have been curtailed or lopped off, the purchasing power of money has decreased, and the Indian civilian or soldier now looks forward to scarcely anything besides his hard-earned pension after a service of 25 to 35 years. Of that pension, the civilian is compelled by Government to contribute fully one-half by monthly subscriptions throughout his service. If he dies, his subscriptions lapse; and it is estimated that the nominal pension of £1000 a year paid to covenanted civil servants, represents a net outlay to Government of under £400 per annum. This cutting down of high salaries is perfectly justified by the modern conditions of Indian service. India is much nearer to England than it was under the Company. An Indian career no longer means a life-long banishment, and Indian officers cannot now expect to be paid for the miseries of an exile which they no longer endure.

I myself believe that if we are to give a really efficient administration to India, many services must be paid for at lower rates even than at present. For those rates are regulated in the higher branches of the administration by the cost of officers brought from England. You cannot work with imported labour as cheaply as you can with native labour, and I regard the more extended employment of the natives not only as an act of justice, but as a financial necessity. Fifty years ago, the natives of India were not capable of conducting an administration according to our English ideas of honesty. During centuries of Mughal rule, almost every rural officer was paid by fees, and every official act had to be purchased. It is difficult to discriminate between fees and bribes, and such a system was in itself sufficient to corrupt the whole administration. It has taken two generations to eradicate this old taint from the Native official mind. But a generation has now sprung up from whose minds it has been eradicated, and who are therefore fitted to take a much larger share in the administration than the Hindus of fifty years ago. I believe that it will be impossible to deny them a larger share in the administration. There are departments, conspicuously those of

Law and Justice, and Finance, in which the natives will more and more supplant the highly-paid imported officials from England. There are other departments, such as the Medical, the Customs, the Telegraph, and the Post Office, in which the working establishments now consist of natives of India, and for which the superintending staff will in a constantly-increasing degree be also recruited from them. The appointment of a few natives annually to the Covenanted Civil Service will not solve the problem. By all means give the natives every facility for entering that service. But the salaries of the Covenanted Service are regulated, not by the rates for local labour, but by the cost of imported officials. If we are to govern the Indian people efficiently and cheaply, we must govern them by means of themselves, and pay for the administration at the market rates for native labour.

We must, however, not only realize this great change which has taken place in the native standard of official morality, we must also realize the great change which has taken place in the physical aspects of administration Fifty years ago, distance played a much more important part in the government of the country than it can now be allowed to play. Each district was as far separated from its neighbours as the three Presidencies are now from one another; and the three Presidencies were practically different countries, requiring completely distinct establishments for their administration. Railways and steamboats have now drawn every part of India closer together, and rendered it possible to control the whole with a smaller superintending staff. For example, the troops in each of the three Presidencies had to be organized as separate armies. This means that there are not only three Commanders-in-Chief in India, but three headquarters' establishments, three Adjutants-General, three Quarter-Masters General, three Surgeons-General, etc., each with his own separate establishment of supervision, and his own separate budget of expenditure. This large outlay was unavoidable when Madras and Bombay were 70 days' march distant from Bengal. But Bombay is now only a 60 hours' railway journey from Calcutta, and steamers leave the Húgli almost daily for Madras. The telegraph connects every part of India, and flashes news in half an hour which formerly would have taken weeks in transmission. The necessity for separate headquarters' establishments for each of the three Presidencies is, therefore, becoming a thing of the past, and economies are now proposed by the Indian Army Commission in this respect.

But while reductions can thus be effected both in the civil administration by the larger employment of natives, and in the military expenditure by re-organizing the three armies in accordance with the altered physical facts of the country, such reductions will not alone suffice to meet the constantly-increasing demands for expenditure. I have shown how the cost of Police, Justice, and Education have more than doubled since the last year of the Company in 1857. The civil administration, as a whole, discloses an equal increase; and, in spite of reductions in certain departments, has risen from 7½ millions sterling in 1857 to 13½ millions net in 1880. The same causes which have led to this increase of expenditure in the past 23 years, will compel a yet further increase in the next 20 years. We now educate 2 millions of pupils in our Indian schools. Before the end of the century, I hope we shall be educating 4 millions. For every square mile now protected by irrigation works, there will then be nearer two square miles. For every native doctor and schoolmaster, there will probably be three. No severity of retrenchment in the civil expenditure, no re-organization of the military establishments, will suffice to meet the outlay thus involved. In India there is a necessity for a steadily increasing revenue, and there is no use in shirking the fact.

How is the additional revenue to be raised? Indian finance ministers have already answered this question. They have shown that it is possible, through the agency of local government, to increase the revenue by means which they would have found it difficult, and perhaps dangerous, to enforce as parts of an Imperial central policy. A great department of Provincial Finance has thus been created since the country passed to the Crown, and now yields a revenue of several millions. As the local demands for improvements in the administration increase, these demands will be met to some extent by local taxation. A tax is a tax, however it may be levied; but in India, as in England, it is possible to do by local rates what it would be very difficult to do by a general impost. In this way, local government in India has obtained an importance which no one would have ventured to predict twenty years ago, and may, before twenty years are over, have become a financial necessity.

While additional resources may thus be hoped for from local taxation, the Imperial revenues have not stood still. Many of their items increase from natural causes. Thus, the land revenue has risen from under 15 millions in 1857 to 18⅗ millions net in 1880. As the population multiplies they consume more salt, more excisable commodities of every sort; and as the trade of the country develops, the revenue from stamps and miscellaneous items increases with it. The revenues of India are by no means stationary, but they do not augment with the same rapidity as the increased demands upon them. Under the Company, almost the whole revenues were supplied by indirect taxation; the Queen's Government has been forced to introduce direct taxation. Forty years ago, a permanent income-tax would have been regarded as a cruel and an unrighteous impost by the British nation. In England, we have only learned to bear an income-tax by slow degrees. Year after year, our fathers were assured that the income-tax was only temporary: we have been constrained to recognise it as one of the most permanent items in our national revenue. The Indian people are now learning the same lesson with equal difficulty. Twenty years ago, the income-tax was introduced into India as a purely temporary measure. Its temporary character has again and again been re-asserted; various disguises have been substituted for it;

but it has now become an established source of Indian revenue. It is an unpopular tax everywhere, but it is especially unpopular in India, where the average income is very small; and where the lower officials, through whom such a tax must be levied, still lie under suspicion of corrupt practices. I believe it is possible to free that taxation from much of its present unpopularity. For its vexatiousness has to a large extent proceeded from its temporary character, and from the necessity of a fresh inquisition into the private affairs of the people on each occasion of its renewal. You cannot expect a host of native underlings to be very honest, when they know that their employment will cease in a few years. But while something may be done to render the income-tax less unpopular, the fact remains that the people of India are now brought face to face with direct taxation.

It may be said that, after all, we take much less revenue than the Native dynasties did. Surely, if the State demands averaged 60 millions sterling during the tumultuous centuries of the Mughal Empire, the country could be made to pay the same amount under our peaceful rule. Yet the actual taxation during the ten years ending 1879 has averaged just 35 millions, and at the present moment, including the new Provincial Rates, it stands at 40 millions. If we were to levy the 80 millions of taxation which Aurangzeb demanded, India would be, financially, the most prosperous country in the world. But she would be, morally and socially, the most miserable. The Mughal Empire wrung its vast revenue out of the people by oppressions which no English minister would dare to imitate. The technical terms of the Native revenue system form themselves a record of extortion and pillage. Among the Marhattas, to collect revenue and to make war was synonymous. Better the poverty of the British Government of India than the Imperial splendours of the Mughals, or the military magnificence of the Marhattas, reared upon the misery of the peasant. In a country where the people are poor, the Government ought to be poor: for it must either be poor or oppressive. The poverty of the Indian people lies at the root of the poverty of the Indian Government.

No financial dexterity will get rid of this fundamental fact. I sometimes see devices proposed for making the Indian Government rich without rendering the Indian people miserable. One of the latest is to relax the so-called rigidity of our finance. This means that we are to calculate the cost of administration over a period of twenty years, and to allow the annual collections to fluctuate according to the harvests; relaxing, when necessary, the demand for individual years, and spreading the deficit over the whole period of twenty years. Such a system is impracticable, for two distinct reasons. In the first place, the tax-payer would never know exactly how much he would have to pay in any year. Revenue-collecting in India would resolve itself into an annual wrangle between the Government officers and the people. This was the state of things under the Mughal Empire. The peasant protested and cried out; the revenue-officer insisted and squeezed; and the victory rested with the most clamorous on the one side, or with the most pitiless on the other. But even after the annual wrangle was over, there would still be an annual necessity of collecting the balance of previous years. It would simply be impossible to collect such balances without the severities which disgraced the early days of the Company, when it took over the Native revenue system and administered by Native officers. The second objection to relaxing the uniformity of the yearly demand, arises from the fact that it would be impossible to vary the uniformity of the yearly expenditure. Punctuality in defraying the charges of Government involves, also, punctuality in realizing its revenues. Under the Mughal Empire, as under the Turkish Empire at present, no large class of officials ever expected to receive regular salaries. They got their pay when they could, and those who threatened loudest got most. When the Treasury ran dry, the officials could always fall back upon the plunder of the people. This irregularity of payment was so deeply impressed upon the Native revenue system, that years after the Company took over Bengal, it ordered as a matter of course, during a time of financial difficulty, that all payments from the Treasury should be suspended, except the cost of dieting the prisoners and the rewards for killing tigers. If the Government of India were now to get six months into arrears with the payment of its servants, it would open the old flood-gates of official extortion, bribery, and fee-levying which it has taken a hundred years of honest rule to dam up. Rigid punctuality in paying one's debts is only possible by means of rigid punctuality in collecting one's dues. Apart from the evils of constant borrowing to meet current outlay, incident to such a plan of relaxing the current taxation, it would strike at the root of the first essential of a good revenue system; namely, the certainty which each man has, as to the amount which he can be called to pay. In place of a regular demand from the tax-payers and regular salaries to the public servants, it would substitute an annual wrangle with the tax-payers, and an annual scramble among the officials.

The rigidity of our Indian system of finance is only one of many difficulties which a Government that tries to do right has to encounter in India. Such an administration is based upon the equality of all its subjects; it has to work among a people steeped in the ideas of caste and of the inequality of races. I shall cite only two illustrations. Twenty-five years ago we were told that railways could never pay in India, because no man of respectable position would sit in the same carriage with a man of low caste. We open our schools to all our Indian subjects, of whatever creed or birth. The Hindus, with their practical genius for adapting themselves to the facts around them, have prospered by a frank acceptance of this system of education. But the upper classes of the Muhammadans, with their pride of race and disdainful creed, have stood aloof, and so fail to qualify themselves for the administration of a country which not long ago they ruled. Ten years ago, in my *Indian Musalmáns*, I pointed out that among 418 gazetted judicial Native officers in Bengal, 341 were Hindus, while only 77 were Muhammadans. The Government took measures to remedy this inequality, and went so far as to supplement its general system of public instruction with sectarian schools and colleges for Muhammadans. But the Musalmán still isolates himself, and out of 504 similar appointments now held by natives, only 53 are filled by Muhammadans. This practically means that while one-third of the population of Lower Bengal are Musalmáns, only one-tenth of the Government patronage falls to them; the other nine-tenths are monopolized by the Hindus. It thus follows that a system of education based upon the equality of the subject results in the practical exclusion of a large section of the population from public employ.

You will now understand how unsafe are those guides who see only the anomalies of our rule without having penetrated into their causes. Such writers tell you that the people of India are very poor, therefore they conclude the Government is to blame. I also tell you that the people of India are very poor, because the population has increased at such a rate as to outstrip, in some parts, the food-producing powers of the land; because every square mile of Bengal has now to support three times as many families as it had to support a hundred years ago; because every square mile of British India, deducting the outlying provinces of Burma and Assam, has to feed nearly three times as many mouths as each square mile of the Native States. Such writers tell you that the soil of India is being exhausted, and that therefore the Government is to blame; that the expenditure is increasing; that the revenues are inelastic; that the rigidity of our taxation bears heavily on the people; and that for each of these and all our other difficulties, the simple and invariable explanation is, that the Government is to blame. I also tell you that the soil is being exhausted; that the requirements for additional expenditure are incessant, while the revenues can with difficulty be increased; and I have tried in each case to tell you honestly the reason why. Such writers tell you, or would tell you if they knew it, that in a single province, under our system of State education, twenty millions of Musalmáns, the former rulers of the country, are practically ousted from public employment, and that therefore the Government must be to blame. Let me answer them in the words in which the leader of the Muhammadan community of Calcutta sums up his most able pamphlet on this exclusion of his countrymen: 'For these figures, however lamentable, I certainly do not lay the blame at the door of Government. The real cause of this unhappy state of things is to be found in the backwardness of the Muhammadans in conforming themselves to the requirements of the times, and thus remaining behind in the race of competition with other nations.'

I only wish that the gentlemen were right who think that all our Indian difficulties are due to the shortcomings of the Government. For if they were right, then I feel sure that England, in the discharge of her high duty, would swiftly sweep away her culpable representatives in India. But, alas! our difficulties there are not susceptible of so easy a cure. Every year England sends to India a picked body of young men from her public schools and universities to recruit the Indian administration. There is not a master in the country, who does not feel honoured when his pupils are thus chosen. For, although the old pecuniary advantages of the Indian Civil Service have very properly been curtailed, that service still forms one of the noblest and most useful careers open to our youth. To an administration thus composed, England sends out, as heads, the ablest statesmen who can be tempted by the emoluments and honours of high Indian office. She supplies India with trained Parliamentary financiers like Mr. James Wilson; with jurists and legislators like Sir Fitzjames Stephen and Sir Henry Sumner Maine; with Governors-General like the iron Dalhousie and the beloved Mayo, from one of her great national parties, and like the wise Minto and the just Northbrook, from the other. I do not see how to improve the English materials of an administration thus selected and thus led. But I do know that, if the easy explanation of all our Indian difficulties were that the Indian Government is to blame, the British nation would very soon substitute a better government for it.

I believe that, in dealing with the difficulties which now confront it, the Government of India must look round for new allies. Those allies will be found among the natives. So long as the administration proceeded upon the English political maxim of *laissez faire* in

India, it was possible to conduct its higher branches, at any rate, by Englishmen. The Company's administration, thus composed, did much. It secured India from external enemies, created internal protection for person and property, and took the first steps in the development of the country. But the good work thus commenced has assumed such dimensions under the Queen's Government of India, that it can no longer be carried on, or even supervised, by imported labour from England, except at a cost which India cannot sustain. While the old duties have extended, new ones have been added. As soon as the English nation began really to interest itself in India, it found that the Government must there take on itself several functions which in England may well be left to private enterprise. In a country where the Government is the sole great capitalist, railways, canals, docks, and commercial works of many sorts had either to be initiated by the Government, or to be left unattempted. The principle of *laissez faire* can, in fact, be safely applied only to self-governing nations. The English in India are now called upon, either to stand by and witness the pitiless overcrowding of masses of hungry human beings, or to aid the people in increasing the food-supply to meet their growing wants. The problem is a difficult one; but I have shown why I believe it capable of solution. Forty years ago, the political economists would have told us that a Government had no right to enter on such problems at all; and forty years hereafter we should have had an Indian Ireland, multiplied fiftyfold, on our hands. The condition of things in India compels the Government to enter on these problems. Their solution, and the constant demand for improvement in the general executive, will require an increasing amount of administrative labour. India cannot afford to pay for that labour at the English rates, which are the highest in the world for official service. But she can afford to pay for it at her own Native rates, which are perhaps the lowest in the world for such employment.

It may be well, therefore, to know what the natives themselves think about the situation. A petition presented to Parliament last session by the British Indian Association sets forth their programme of reform. It asks for a more independent share in the legislative councils of India; and it is certain that at no distant date such a share must be conceded to the Indian people. It urges the necessity of military retrenchments, and the injustice of dealing with the Indian finances in the party interests of England rather than in the sole interest of the Indian tax-payer. At this moment, retrenchments to the extent of, I am told, 1½ millions are being proposed by the Indian Army Commission; and there is no doubt that Indian finance has been sometimes handled with an eye to English rather than to Indian interests. It asks, to touch only on the principal heads, for the more extended employment of the natives; and I believe a more extended employment of them to be not only an act of justice, but a financial necessity. The number of Europeans employed in the higher civil offices had been reduced in all the provinces of the Bengal Presidency from 929 in 1874 to 838 in 1879, and the Government has now a scheme under consideration for further reducing them to 571.

The Native petition asks for a Commission of Enquiry, similar to those great Parliamentary Committees which sat every twentieth year in the time of the Company to examine into its administration. I am compelled as a student of Indian history, to acknowledge that each successive period of improvement under the Company took its rise from one of these inquests. The Parliamentary Enquiry of 1813 abolished the Company's Indian trade, and compelled it to direct its whole energies in India to the good government of the people. The Charter Act of 1833 opened up that government to the natives of India irrespective of caste, creed, or race. The Act of 1853 abolished the patronage by which the Company filled up the higher branches of its service, and laid down the principle that the administration of India was too national a concern to be left to the chances of benevolent nepotism; and that England's representatives in India must be chosen openly and without favour from the youth of England. The natives now desire that a similar enquiry should be held into the administration of India during the two-and-twenty years since it passed to the Crown. It may perhaps be deemed expedient to postpone such an enquiry till after the next census. Remember we have only had one enumeration of the Indian people. A single census forms, as I have keenly felt while writing these chapters, a very slender basis for the economical problems with which a Commission would have to deal. The Indian administration has nothing to fear, and it may have much to learn, from an enquiry into its work. It is, perhaps, the only administration in the world which has no interest in perpetuating itself. No Indian civilian has the smallest power to secure for son or nephew a place in the service to which he himself belongs. And I feel sure that, if it were found that India could be better administered on some new system, the Indian Civil Service would give its utmost energies to carry out the change.

The Native petition also asks that the recent restrictions on the liberty of the Press should be removed. 'The Indian Press spoke out the truth,' Mr. Gladstone said in Mid-Lothian, 'what was the true mind of the people of India; so that while the freedom of the vernacular Press is recommended in India by all the considerations which recommend it in England, there are other considerations besides. We can get at the minds of people here by other means than the Press. They can meet and petition, and a certain number of them can vote. But in India their meetings and petitioning are comparatively ineffective, while the power of voting is there unknown. The Press was the only means the Government had of getting at the sentiments of the Indian people.'

There is one thing more for which the natives ask, and that is representative institutions for India. I believe that such institutions will, before long, not only be possible but necessary, and that at this moment an electoral body is being developed in India by the municipalities and local district boards. There are already 1163 elected members in the municipal bodies of the Bengal and Madras Presidencies alone. The legislative councils of the Imperial and local Governments have each a Native element in their composition, which although nominated, is fairly chosen so as to represent the various leading classes of the people. Thus of the ten members of the Bengal Council, three are covenanted civilians, one is a Crown lawyer, two are non-official Europeans, and four natives. Of the natives, the first is the editor of the *Hindu Patriot*, the chief Native paper in India; the second is the head of the Muhammadan community in Calcutta; the other two represent the landed and important rural interests. It will not be easy to work representative institutions, and it will be very easy to be misled by them. In the first place, England must make up her mind that, in granting such institutions to the Indian people, she is parting to some extent with her control over India. In the second place, we must proceed upon Native lines, rather than on those paper constitutions for India which English writers love to manufacture. What we want at the present stage, is a recognition of the end to be attained, not an unanimity as to any particular scheme for attaining it.

We must carefully consider the Native solutions for the problem; and I think we may learn a lesson from the practical and moderate character of the Native demands. The *Hindu Patriot* lately expressed those demands in three feasible proposals. First, the extension of the elective principle to all first-class municipalities of British India. Second, the concession to the municipal boards of the three Presidency towns, and a few other great Indian cities, of the right to elect members to the Legislative Councils. Third, the extension of the scope of those Councils, so as to include questions of finance. There would still be the representation of rural India to be provided for by nomination or otherwise. It has taken ten centuries to make the British Constitution, and we must not try to build up one for India in a day. Meanwhile, I can only repeat what I said in 1879 at Birmingham on this point:—'I do not believe that a people numbering one-sixth of the whole inhabitants of the globe, and whose aspirations have been nourished from their earliest youth on the strong food of English liberty, can be permanently denied a voice in the government of their country. I do not believe that races, among whom we raise a taxation of 35 millions sterling, and into whom we have instilled the maxim of "No taxation without representation," as a fundamental right of a people, can be permanently excluded from a share in the management of their finances. I do not believe it practicable to curtail, for long, the right of the freest criticism on their rulers, to 191 millions of British subjects, who have the speeches of our great English statesmen at this moment ringing in their ears.'

Administrative improvements can do much, but the Indian people themselves can do more. The poverty of certain parts of India is the direct and inevitable result of the over-population of those parts of India. The mass of the husbandmen are living in defiance of economic laws. A people of small cultivators cannot be prosperous if they marry irrespective of the means of subsistence, and allow their numbers to outstrip the food-producing powers of the soil. Now that the sword is no longer allowed to do its old work, they must submit to prudential restraints on marriage, or they must suffer hunger. Such restraints have been imperative upon races of small cultivators since the days when Plato wrote his *Republic.* The natives must also equalize the pressure on the soil, by distributing themselves more equally over the country. There is plenty of fertile land in India still awaiting the plough. The Indian husbandman must learn to mobilize himself, and to migrate from the overcrowded provinces to the under-peopled ones. But prudential restraints upon marriage and migration, or emigration, are repugnant alike to the religious customs, and to the most deeply-seated feelings of the Indian husbandman. Any general improvement in these respects must be a work of time. All we can do is to shorten that time by giving the amplest facilities for labour-transport, for education, for manufactures, mining enterprise, and trade. Meanwhile, Government must throw itself into the breach, by grappling with the necessity for an increased and a better distributed food-supply. Changes in the marriage customs, and migrations to new provinces, now opposed by all the traditions of the past, will be forced by the pressure of circumstances upon no distant generation of the Indian people. Every year, thousands of new pupils are gathered into our schools, those pestles and mortars for the superstitions and priestcraft of India. English writers who tell our Indian fellow-subjects to look to the Government for every improvement in their lot, are doing a very great dis-service to the Indian races. The permanent remedies for the poverty of India rest with the people themselves.

But while the Indian Government can do much, and the Indian people can do more, there are some unfulfilled functions which Englishmen in England must with greater fidelity perform. They must realize that the responsibility for India has passed into the hands of Parliament, and through Parliament to the electoral body of Great Britain. They must realize that if, through ignorance or indifference, they fail to discharge that responsibility, they are acting as bad citizens. They must therefore set themselves to learn more about India; they must act in a spirit of absolute honesty towards the Indian finances; and they must deal with Indian questions sent home for their decision, not in the interests of powerful classes or political parties in England, but in the sole interest of the Indian people. I believe that important questions of this sort will before long be submitted to Parliament. When that time comes, if any remembrance of this little book lingers among my countrymen, I hope it may make them more alive to their responsibilities to India, and the more earnest to do their duty by the Indian people.